SOFT FURNISHINGS
ROOM BY ROOM

SOFT FURNISHINGS
ROOM BY ROOM

BETTERWAY BOOKS
CINCINNATI, OHIO

Front cover photographs: (top left): Eaglemoss/Graham Rae
(top centre): VNU/Ariadne Magazine
(top right): VNU/Knippie Idee Magazine
(main): Eaglemoss/Steve Tanner.

Page 3: Eaglemoss/Graham Rae, page 5: Eaglemoss/Lizzie Orme
page 6: Eaglemoss/George Taylor

First published in North America
in 2000 by Betterway Books
an imprint of F&W Publications, Inc.
1507 Dana Avenue
Cincinnati, OH 45207
1-800/289-0963

ISBN 1-55870-576-7

Printed in Hong Kong

10 9 8 7 6 5 4 3 2 1

Contents

Rope tiebacks

*Versatile accessories for any room, rope tiebacks add detail,
color and texture to even the plainest pair of curtains – the
final touch that adds that well-dressed look.*

Most rooms benefit from the maximum amount of natural light that they can get – especially the living room – so looping your curtains back to clear the window makes sense, and also gives you the chance to show off the fabric in elegantly draped folds. You can achieve a subtle, complementary effect by using tiebacks in the same color as your curtains; or you can coordinate the tiebacks with other colors in the room. Chunky and plain, or elaborately tasseled, rope tiebacks are as varied as the curtains they partner, so choose carefully to complement both your fabric and style of window treatment.

▼ *Make the most of a decorative tassel by positioning it off-center along the cord, so that it lies on the face, rather than the edge, of the curtain. Here, to give an 'antiqued' look, the curtains and tiebacks have been stained with a solution of tea (see Here's How on page 9).*

Types of tiebacks

The simplest version is a single strand of thick rope, with the ends neatly netted and finished with cord loops to slip over the hooks. Neat and discreet, this style is ideal for an elegant room, as it holds the curtains in place without dominating the window. Thick cord doubled into a central knot makes a decorative tieback, useful for many window treatments. It works well with both plain and patterned fabrics, especially stripes and checks.

Tassel tiebacks have either a single tassel or a pair, usually attached at a central knot of rope, with equal loops of rope extending at either side. The size and style of tassels varies enormously, giving an inspiring selection of elegantly pretty or imposingly heavy tiebacks. It's important to match the size and weight to the purpose: thick, textured curtain fabrics, like velvet or chenille, or full-length drapes, are well-matched with heavy rope or detailed tassels, to balance the proportions. Delicate, single tassels are just the right touch for sheer fabrics, although you can make a striking contrast of texture by looping armfuls of muslin or voile into thick, tasseled ropes.

▲ *The crunchy, natural texture of a jute tieback forms an interesting contrast to the tailored look of this striped curtain. The rich beige of the jute links to the warm tones in the fabric.*

▲ *Try unusual materials for the tassel to go with a rope tieback. Here corn and shaped wood give a rustic feel, complementing the patterned curtain.*

Rope and tassel tiebacks are made from a wide variety of materials – so look out for different textural qualities to enhance your fabrics. Soft cotton, string, jute and raffia, either undyed or in muted tones, are all perfect for the natural effects popular in today's modern interiors. For a more sumptuous effect, choose textures with a sheen, such as rayon, silk or mercerised cotton.

For a really grand, dramatic statement, perfect for a plush sitting room, you can make bulky, outsized tassels from wool or chenille. Metallic threads are also popular for adding a glamorous glint to a richly colored tassel. Some modern designs may also have shapely heads made from wood, which can be polished, painted, stained or gilded.

Anatomy of a tassel

Each tassel consists of three basic parts – the head, neck and skirt – with design variations worked around this theme.
The head of the tassel is usually a ball shape, covered with yarn, sometimes with a netted or trellised effect on top in a matching or contrasting color.
The neck is the narrow part, tightly wound with yarn, often with one or two decorative ruffs of looped yarn above or below it.
The skirt is the main part of the tassel, which may be a thick bunch of similar threads cut to an equal length, or a combination of different colors and textures. Some tassels have a second skirt of tiny multiple tassels or pompons.

◀ *Plain russet cord tiebacks, positioned unconventionally up to the heading, sweep these formal curtains back to allow the maximum amount of light into the room. The cord trim is repeated dramatically across the base of the goblet-pleated heading.*

Positioning tassels

To make the most of an impressive, decorative tassel, make sure that it lies on the face of the curtain, rather than on the very edge. You can do this either by fitting two tieback hooks for each tieback, or by pulling the back cord loop of the tieback so that it is slightly longer, allowing the tassel to sit at the front of the curtain.

Alternatively, to draw attention to the back edge rather than the front edge of the curtain – perhaps to accentuate a wallpaper border or a decorative hook – just pull the back loop until the front one is very short, so that the tassel hangs next to the hook.

▲ *From plush chenille to crunchy twisted cotton, the huge variety of tiebacks available means there's one to suit everyone's taste.*

Even the hooks from which you hang your tiebacks can be a design feature. There's a huge range to choose from, with decorative details from teddy bears to Celtic knots, in a range of materials to match your curtain pole. Make sure the hooks are big enough to take the cord loops of the tieback.

HERE'S HOW

Antiquing your curtains and tiebacks

Give inexpensive cotton curtains and rope tiebacks an antiqued look by staining them with a strong solution of tea. Dye the fabric before using it to make curtains to allow for shrinkage.

You'll need a container large enough to hold the fabric plus liquid to cover it – a plastic dustbin is ideal for large amounts. For the dye, mix a solution of one part strong tea, made with tea leaves, to two parts hot water – as a guide, 1.5kg (3lb) of tea is enough to stain about 6m (6½yd) of fabric. Leave to soak overnight, then rinse lightly to remove tea leaves. Dye cotton rope tiebacks in the same way; leave to drip-dry.

Complete the look by painting your brass curtain accessories with French enamel varnish to give an authentically tarnished finish.

Creative ideas

You can use rope tiebacks for a purely decorative effect, as design details to highlight all sorts of window treatments, or to play a more functional role, to hold your drapes in place. Use the tieback as it is, or unravel the knot of one with single or double tassels to give a versatile length of rope with tasseled ends; attract attention to a beautiful pole or curtain heading, for example, by tying the rope around the pole, leaving the tassel to hang beside the curtain heading. Another option is to thread it in among the folds of a scarf drape, giving extra texture and color.

Tied into a bow, a rope tieback can be used to highlight the meeting point between two swags in a formal arrangement. Alternatively, for a more theatrical, dramatic look, use two pairs of tiebacks – one above the other – on a long, full pair of curtains, dressed carefully to frame the window in cascading folds of fabric.

Rope-style tiebacks look just as good around a bed as they do at the window. Use rope and tassel tiebacks to loop up corona or half-tester curtains – they allow the fabric to drape very softly round the bed, looping forward into the room to enclose the head board for a cosy, romantic feel. To achieve the best effects, remember to match the color, weight and texture of the tieback with that of the curtain fabric.

▲ *Nestling in between the meeting point of two curtains, and backlit by the window, a double-tasseled tieback creates an unexpected focal point.*

▼ *Tiebacks work to balance this asymmetrical display. One holds the single curtain back from the window, while the other fills the space left at the top.*

◄ *To counteract the fixed heading of this curtain, which cannot be drawn across, two tiebacks ensure that light finds its way into the room. The drapery is carefully arranged to create a scalloped effect down the window.*

Pompons

*A pompon fringe – tiny tufted balls of yarn strung in an ordered
row from a braid heading – is an all-time favorite trimming. Use it to
add an enchanting and light-hearted flourish to soft furnishings.*

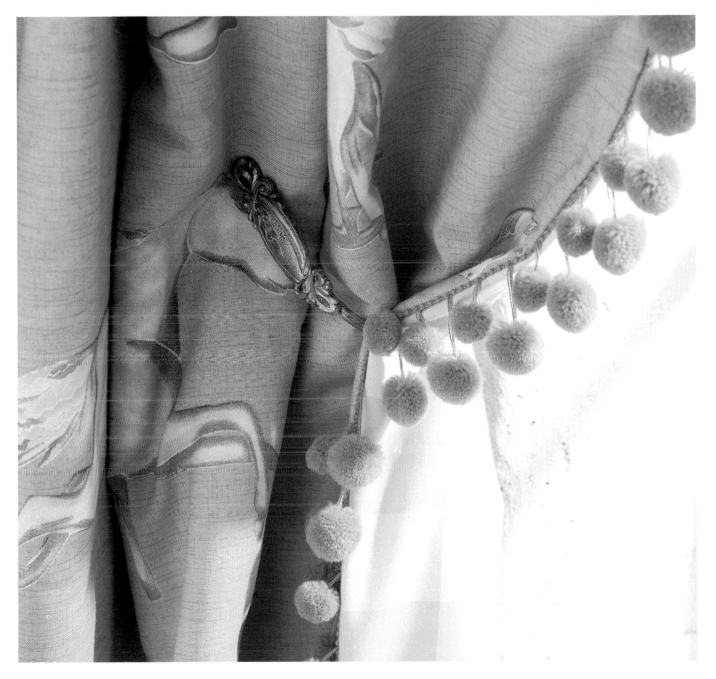

Pompons and pompon fringes are enjoying renewed popularity as trimmings, and it's easy to understand why. The textural, must-touch quality of individual pompons and the bobbing of the whimsical, almost humorous fringe made from miniature versions are both hard to resist.

Almost all forms of soft furnishings benefit from this versatile trim. The delightful pompon fringe, or bobble fringing as it is sometimes known, is a lively edging for curtains, pelmets, tiebacks, tablecloths, lampshades and shelves. Individual pompons, which you can make in any diameter, with a mixture of colors in a single tufted ball if you wish, rival tassels as glamorous trims for tiebacks, pelmets, bell pulls and cushions.

While you can easily make individual pompons from wool, it is simpler to

▲ *Pompons literally dance along the leading edge of a curtain. The trim is inserted between the main fabric and lining as the curtain is made up.*

buy pompon fringe by the meter (yard) from soft-furnishing departments and fabric or craft stores. The edging is available in a tantalizing array of colors and styles.

The versatile trim

Surprisingly, pompon fringing suits a wide range of room styles, from opulent Victorian and period-style schemes through to light-hearted contemporary rooms, in rich, deep colors, zingy brights or understated neutrals.

For the best results, match the weight and color of the pompon fringe to the item it is trimming. A multi-layered burgundy edging, for instance, adds a luxurious embellishment to floor-length brocade curtains, while simple white bobbles are ideally suited to diaphanous voile drapes. Dyed in bright primary shades, a basic pompon fringe is a winner in a child's bedroom.

When you go to buy the trim, if you can't see what you want on display, it is worth asking the sales assistant if there are any sample books. Many fabric manufacturers produce ranges of pompon fringes to complement their fabric and trimming collections, so you may be able to order the one you want.

Make it yourself

You can recapture the essential fun look of a pompon trim by making individual pompons. Although very easy to make, they are time consuming (allow about half an hour for each pompon),

so it's best to make larger ones and use them sparingly. Just one pompon strategically placed at each edge of a cushion, say, has as much impact as a complete edging.

When you make your own pompons, they are a perfect way of using up lengths of leftover yarns. You can wind any knitting or tapestry wool, knitting cotton or even string and raffia into a pompon – the thicker the yarn the quicker the pompon takes shape. For original and unusual effects, there is no reason why you can't mix yarns and colors in a single pompon.

Applying pompons

You can stitch most pompon fringes in place either by hand or machine, incorporating them quite easily into a seam or simply attaching them along the edge of an existing item. There are no-sew options, too. Using a clear craft or fabric adhesive, you can stick pompons along the lower edge of a blind, pelmet or lampshade, or to the front of a shelf.

You can also handstitch or glue individual pompons, cut from a length of braid or made by hand, in place. Single pompons look very effective defining the points of a shaped edge, such as a pelmet.

▲ *To show off the pompon fringe to best effect, sweep the curtains away from the window with holdbacks or tiebacks.*

◄ *When you set a pompon fringe into the seam of a cushion cover, it appears as if each pompon has been individually attached. To recreate this effect, you need to make up the cover from scratch. If you want to add a fringe to an existing or ready-made cover, just handstitch it in place using matching thread.*

▲ Strategically placed individual pompons – in this case one at each corner of a cushion cover – have enormous decorative impact.

▲ The delights of a colorful pompon fringe are well displayed in free fall around the base of a small lampshade.

▶ Put remnants of wool to good use by making your own pompon fringe. Here, small, multicolored pompons are attached to a twisted rope of wool, creating a wonderful trim for a travel rug.

◀ *Snow-white pompons and voile add a frivolous air at this window. It's practical too – the sheer curtain provides instant privacy when lifted off the holdback.*

▼ *Adding a decorative trim is a simple way to rejuvenate existing soft furnishings. Here, a bobble fringe, overlaid with a sage and gold braid, is glued to the lower edge of a Roman blind.*

Making pompons

Pompons are easy to make – all you need are two card hoops, some yarn, a pair of scissors and a tapestry needle.

HERE'S HOW

1 Preparing the hoops Cut two circles of card to the desired pompon size, then cut a smaller circle, about a third of the diameter of the outer one, in the center of each card.

2 Winding wool Use balls of yarn small enough to pass through the central hole. Holding card hoops together, wind yarn around them, tying in loose ends. Keep winding until central circle is full, using a tapestry needle to thread yarn when ball no longer fits through center.

3 Finishing pompon Push scissors between the two hoops and cut yarn around edges. Tie a length of yarn tightly between hoops to hold cut threads. Cut away card, then fluff out pompon. Trim off straggly ends, leaving the tied threads long for attaching the pompon.

Homing in on buttons

*With a few buttons or self-cover button bases in your
sewing kit, you need never be at a loss for a good trimming idea
to liven up a range of soft furnishings.*

Whether you use them as practical fasteners or purely decorative devices, buttons are a wonderfully simple way of coordinating a room scheme or introducing original details. Just as buttons make stylish, inexpensive fashion accessories, so they are useful for adding that eye-catching twist or focal point on chairs, cushions and curtains. Featuring buttons on soft furnishings in your home only goes to show that the simplest design ideas are very often the smartest.

Your choice and arrangement of the buttons are important. Depending on the situation, there's a place for buttons that are large or small, colorful or clear, shiny or fabric-covered, round or unusually shaped. You can place them singly or in groups, to match or contrast with the surrounding fabric – or even use an assortment of sizes or colors on the same

▲ *Like two jolly fabric dominoes, a couple of stylish button-decorated cushions stand out from the crowd. Rows of wool tufted buttons perk up the blue cushion, while a cross of black and gold buttons contrasts boldly with the orange cover.*

item for a zany effect. So, just choose your buttons, decide on a design strategy, thread your needle and start buttoning.

Making buttons work

Conventionally, buttons are practical fasteners, used in conjunction with buttonholes or fabric loops, to keep flaps closed or edges together. However, ordinary fashion buttons also look very effective when attached to all manner of soft furnishings, as inexpensive decorations in their own right. Alternatively, you can use buttons in a formal structural way with buttoning, to give upholstery on chairs, sofas and gusseted cushions an invitingly plump and springy appearance.

Popular in Victorian times, buttoning is a special technique in which buttons are stitched tightly into the padding, partly to hold it in place and partly to exaggerate its luxurious overstuffed depth.

Generally, formal buttoning is done with fabric-covered buttons. You can buy various sizes of easy-to-cover plastic or metal button bases with shanks in fabric or craft stores. The metal varieties are stronger and better for soft furnishings. When covering your own buttons, it's always worth making a spare, just in case one gets lost.

▲ *Ordinary shirt buttons perform admirably as conventional fasteners on a whole host of home accessories. Here, little pearly and color-coordinated ones are working in harmony with fabric loops to hold the flaps of two cushion covers closed.*

◀ *The deeply buttoned back of this armchair demonstrates a classic device for sculpting and securing the upholstery, while emphasizing its ample padding. Here, matching fabric-covered buttons nestle into the upholstery; covered in a contrasting color, say red, they would emerge more boldly.*

Gusset cushions

*Made-to-measure gusset cushions add simple tailored style
and comfort to hard chairs, and are ideal for transforming
garden chairs and benches into stylish indoor seating.*

Gusset cushions are made from two fabric pieces which form the top and bottom of the cushion, joined with a fabric strip (the gusset), which runs around the circumference and creates a boxy effect. The cushion is filled with a foam pad, cut to the same size as the cover – upholstery suppliers will cut a foam pad to the required size for your cushion. To enable the pad to be removed easily, a zipper is inserted in one side of the gusset strip, which extends slightly around the adjoining corners.

Gusset cushions may be square, rectangular or round, and are sometimes shaped to accommodate chair arms. The steps on the following pages show how to make a square or rectangular cushion, with piped seamlines, but you can easily adapt them to suit your own requirements.

If using a patterned fabric, try to match the design across the top piece and gusset strip – especially along the front of the cushion. Geometrics, such as stripes and checks, suit the boxy shape of gusset cushions.

▲ *Colorful gusset cushions provide comfortable seating on these unusual wooden benches. Team with contrasting scatter cushions for added comfort and style.*

Making a gusset cushion

You will need

- ◆ Furnishing fabric
- ◆ Piping cord, fabric to cover piping cord
- ◆ Foam cushion pad
- ◆ Zipper, 20cm (8in) longer than back of foam pad
- ◆ Matching sewing thread
- ◆ Tape measure, pins
- ◆ Machine piping and zipper foot

Measuring and cutting out

Top and bottom pieces Measure the width and length of the foam pad, and add 2.5cm (1in) to each measurement for seam allowances. Cut two fabric pieces to this size.

Gusset strip Measure the depth of the foam pad, and add 2.5cm (1in). Cut a fabric strip to this width by the length of the cushion front plus twice the length of the cushion side.

Zipper gusset strips Cut two fabric strips, the length of the zipper tape by half the depth of the foam pad plus 2.5cm (1in) for seams.

Piping Cut bias fabric strips, 4cm (1½in) wide, to go twice around the cushion, plus extra for seam allowances and ease.

1 Putting in the zipper Press under a 1.3cm (½in) seam allowance on one long edge of each zipper strip. Position the folded edges of the strips along the center of the zipper teeth and pin. Using a piping foot, topstitch 1cm (⅜in) from the folds to hold the zipper in place.

2 Working the gusset strip Press under 5cm (2in) on one short edge of the gusset strip. Overlap the zipper strip to cover the zipper tape. Stitch through all layers 4cm (1½in) from the folded edge of the gusset strip. Edgestitch along the fold to within 2.5cm (1in) of the centered zipper.

3 Adding the piping Cover the piping cord, and pin it around the edges of the top and bottom cushion pieces, with right sides facing and edges matching; snip into the piping at the corners for ease. Using a zipper foot, stitch the piping in place.

4 Joining gusset to cushion top Right sides together, pin the gusset strip to the cushion top, centering the zipper along the back edge and snipping into the corners for ease. Starting 2.5cm (1in) from the raw short edge, stitch the gusset in place; stop 10cm (4in) from the starting stitches. Adjust the unsewn edges to fit the top. Stitch ends together. Trim excess fabric. Finish stitching the gusset strip to the cushion top.

5 Completing the cushion Fold the gusset strip and snip the seam allowance to mark the bottom corner positions. Open the zipper. With right sides together, pin the gusset strip to the cushion bottom, matching the snips in the gusset to the corners of the bottom piece. Stitch the seam, then turn the cover right side out. Insert the pad and close the zipper.

Simple stool cover

*Update your color scheme or give
a battered stool a fresh lease of life with
a streamlined new cover.*

A footstool is heaven when your feet are throbbing after a long day; small stools and ottomans are handy for extra seating, too. They also make useful occasional tables – somewhere to put a tray of tea or a stack of books. They're just the sort of thing you can pick up secondhand for next-to-nothing, but they'll definitely need a facelift to look fresh and bright. It's very useful to have a removable and washable cover, especially if you choose a pale color scheme.

This neat model will disguise an old upholstered stool perfectly, and the uncomplicated shape and simple lines are in tune with modern streamlined interiors. The cover is made from a single piece of fabric, pleated at the corners and fastened with eyelets tied through with cord – an important detail. You could use the same idea to cover a chest or wooden box. To soften the hard lines of a box add a layer of lightweight batting and lining.

To make the cover, choose a furnishing fabric that has enough body to retain the shape. Also check that the fabric is dense enough to stop the original color showing through; this is particularly important if you are adding a pale cover over a dark one. Make sure that the fabric is washable; as the cover opens out almost flat it will be easy to wash and press. The cover looks neat and smart in stripes or cheerful checks, but a bright splashy floral would work well for a fresh look. For a more traditional room, choose a cotton damask. You may be able to select the eyelets for color, too: cool chrome for a modern look and brass for a warmer color scheme and traditional fabrics.

◄ *Pleated corners fastened with cords threaded through eyelets make the stool cover easy to remove for cleaning.*

Making the stool cover

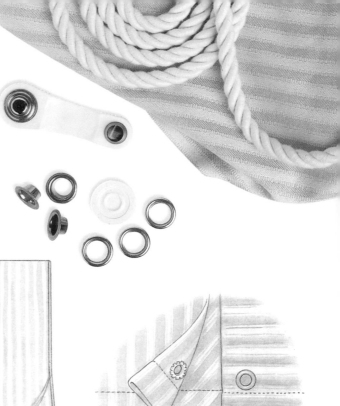

You will need

◆ **Fabric**

◆ **Matching thread**

◆ **Eight large eyelets and applicator**

◆ **3.2m (3½yd) non-fray rope or cord**

1 Cutting out Measure centrally across stool and down to the floor at each side. Then measure across the opposite direction in same way. Add 8cm (3¼in) to the measurement for hems and cut fabric to this size.

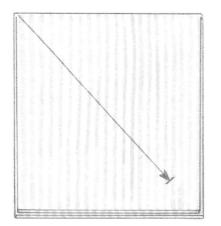

2 Marking corners Fold the fabric in half then half again. Measure from the floor up one corner of the stool then diagonally across to opposite corner and back down to the floor. Divide this measurement in half and add 4cm (1½in) for the hem. Mark this distance out from center of fabric towards opposite corner.

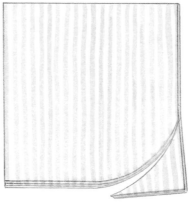

3 Trimming corners Link the mark with a curved line to join straight edges about 5-10cm (2-4in) less than height of stool away from the corner. Trim along marked line. Trim all corners the same.

4 Stitching hem Press 1cm (⅜in) then 3cm (1¼in) to the wrong side, easing in fullness around curves. Tack hem. Drape the cover over the stool to check the fit and the corners. Adjust if necessary, then machine stitch hem in place.

5 Forming pleats Replace cover on stool and arrange in an inverted pleat at the base of each corner to take out the fullness. Pleat each corner the same. Pin through the double layer of each pleat to mark its position.

6 Attaching eyelets Remove cover from stool and make an eyelet through the double layer of each pleat just above the hem. Ensure each time that the good side of the eyelet is on the side of the pleat which will show.

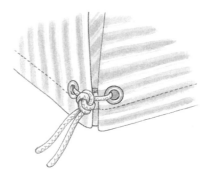

7 Tying the cords Cut cord or rope to make four 80cm (31½in) lengths. If required, apply liquid fray-check to ends of cord to prevent unravelling. Place cover on stool. Thread cord or rope through the eyelets and knot ends at the front of pleats.

EYELETS

Tip

When applying eyelets, place them on a solid surface such as a concrete floor or paving slab. A table or wooden floor will often 'give' as you hammer the applicator, making it difficult to apply the eyelet.

Circular tablecloths

*An ordinary round table looks instantly more presentable
when covered with an easy-to-make circular cloth. You can leave the
hem plain or add a flourish with a fringed or frilled trim.*

Covering a round occasional table with a cloth is an ideal way of introducing a new fabric into a scheme. It's also an economical solution for hiding an old table so that it can play a new role as an occasional table in the living room.

You may already have a round table that has seen better days, or you can hunt for a suitable candidate in a secondhand store. Alternatively, you can buy an inexpensive chipboard kit version, designed to be covered with a cloth, that you assemble yourself. Such tables are readily available in a range of diameters from DIY stores or by mail order from magazines.

You can make a round tablecloth to cover a table of any size. For a large cloth, you may want to avoid the extra expense of lining it, although a lining gives the finished cloth extra body and

▲ *The advantage of making your own soft furnishings is that you can coordinate your room scheme. In this case, the round tablecloth not only matches the upholstery but disguises an old table at the same time.*

a more luxurious appearance. To hide the table underneath, the cloth must hang to the floor. You can lengthen a short cloth with a frill or deep fringing.

Making a plain cloth

The simplest round cloth is machine hemmed around the edge, but for a neater edge you should hem it by hand. Add a lining for a more luxurious look.

Estimating fabric amounts

For most round cloths, you need more than one width of fabric and have to join widths. Work out the diameter of the cloth (**C**), following step 1 below. Compare this with the width of your fabric. If the diameter of the cloth is one to two fabric widths wide, you need to buy a length of fabric double the diameter. If the diameter is more than twice the fabric width, you need a fabric length three times the diameter.

When joining widths, attach them on either side of a full central width to avoid a ridged seam in the middle.

You will need

- Fabric
- Tape measure
- Pattern paper
- Drawing pin, string and pencil
- Scissors
- Lining fabric (optional)
- Matching thread

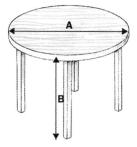

1 Working out the cloth diameter Measure the diameter of the table top (**A**) and the drop (**B**) from the top of the table to the floor. For the diameter of the cloth (**C**), add twice **B** to **A**, plus 4cm (1½in) for the hem.

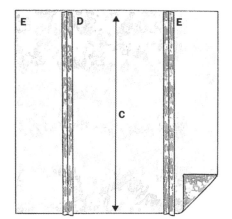

2 Joining widths *For two widths,* cut the fabric in half widthways. Use one piece as the central panel (**D**). Cut the other piece in half lengthways and, with right sides together, stitch one half (**E**) to either side of central panel. Neaten then press seams open. *For three widths,* cut length in three and join long edges.

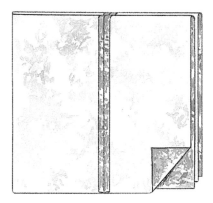

3 Preparing paper pattern Fold fabric into quarters, matching outer edges and seams. Cut out a square of paper to this size. Working on a suitable surface, push a drawing pin into one corner of the paper.

Tip

SOFT FINISH
To soften the edges of the table top and protect the surface, cut a circle from an old blanket or piece of interlining, a few centimeters (inches) larger in diameter than the table, and spread it out under the cloth.

◄ *The tablecloth need not reach to the floor. If an occasional table has an interesting base that complements the room's decor, a shorter cloth may be a better option.*

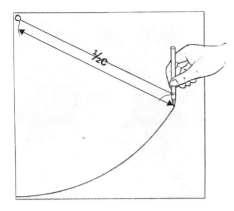

4 Drawing circular pattern Wrap one end of a length of string around a pencil and the other end around the drawing pin so that the length of the taut string is the radius of the table cloth (½**C**). Holding the pencil upright, draw a quarter circle on the paper.

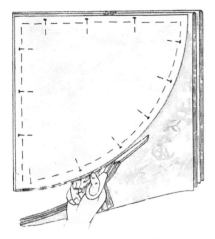

5 Cutting out the fabric Pin the paper pattern to the folded fabric matching the right angle corner to the center fabric fold. Cut the fabric through all thicknesses, along the drawn paper pattern line. (With a bulky or slippery fabric cut through just two layers at once, having tacked the pattern to the fabric.) Open out the fabric circle and press flat.

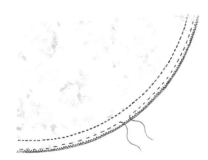

6 Preparing the hem Neaten the outer edge of the hem with machine zigzag stitch. For a smooth hem edge, machine stitch all around the circle 2cm (¾in) from the outer edge. To take up the hem fullness, stitch a row of gathering 6mm (¼in) from outer edge, stopping and starting the stitching at the four quarter points.

7 Turning up the hem Press under the hem allowance so that the stitching line, 2cm (¾in) from edge, falls on the wrong side, close to the fold. Gently pull up the gathering thread to smooth out the hem and pin in place.

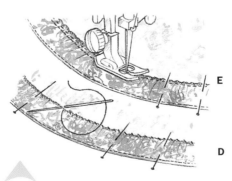

8 Hemming the cloth If you are not lining the cloth, hand slipstitch the hem (**D**) for a neat finish. For a quicker alternative, machine stitch the hem close to the neatened edge and parallel to the folded edge (**E**).

▲ *Putting one tablecloth on top of another is an effective decorating device. Here, the striped undercloth sweeps to the ground to hide the table underneath, while the smaller square cutwork cloth is displayed to advantage on top.*

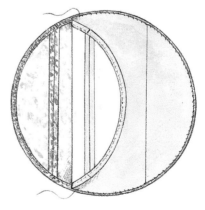

9 Lining the cloth (optional) Omit step **8**. Cut a circle of lining the same size as the fabric, joining widths if necessary. Turn up a 2.5cm (1in) hem as in step **6**, without the zigzag finish. With wrong sides facing, pin the lining to the fabric and slipstitch hems together. Press, checking the lining doesn't roll to the right side.

Frilled tablecloth

A pretty frill emphasizes the swirling folds of the tablecloth and provides a chance to introduce a coordinating plain color or complementary pattern.

A frilled cloth may be a more economical alternative if it allows you to cut the main circle from one width of fabric. Then you can use a coordinating fabric remnant for the frill.

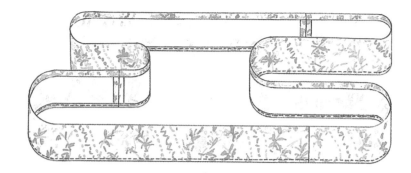

1 Measuring up Decide on the depth of the frill. Subtract the depth of the frill from the overhang measurement (**B**), and add 2cm (¾in) for the hem. Make a basic circular cloth following the instructions on pages 22–23.

2 Cutting the frill Measure around the base of the cloth to find its circumference and double the measurement. Cut strips across the width of the fabric to make up this measurement by the frill depth plus 6cm (2¼in) for hems and seams.

3 Preparing the frill Right sides together, join short ends of frill strips to form a circle. Neaten, then press seams open. Turn under, press and stitch a 1.5cm (⅝in) double hem along the lower edge. Neaten top edge by pressing under a 3cm (1¼in) hem.

4 Stitching the gathering Run two rows of parallel gathering stitches 1.5cm (⅝in) and 2.5cm (1in) from the pressed edge of the frill ring through both layers. For even gathering, stop and start the stitching at intervals around the circle.

▼ *A frill is a good way of lengthening a cloth. The frill on this cloth is part of the overall fabric design.*

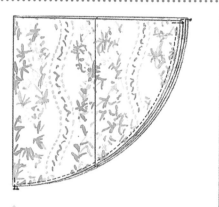

5 Marking the frill and cloth Fold the cloth in quarters and mark the edge folds with pins. Lay the frill flat and fold in half. Mark the four folds with pins on the top edge.

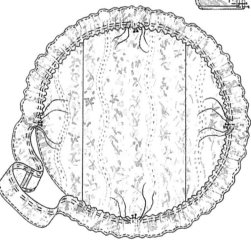

6 Attaching the frill Matching marker pins, place wrong side of frill on right side of cloth, overlapping frill top edge by 3cm (1¼in). Pin the frill to the cloth, pulling up the gathering stitches evenly to make it fit. Working from the front, machine stitch through all layers, between the rows of gathering. Remove gathering threads.

Random appliqué rug

Treat your feet and your eyes with this sensually textured rug. Combining an exciting range of pile fabrics, roughly cut strips are appliquéd together to create a unique design.

This interesting rug combines good looks with economy; you can use up offcuts and remnant bargains for the randomly cut strips. For this version, we've chosen a range of luxuriously soft, pile fabrics, from richly colored velvets to jazzy fur fabrics, but you could make a very different looking rug with the various fabrics used through your room scheme – florals, plains, and checked cottons, for example, in toning colors, or a mixture of differently textured creams and beiges.

The backing and border are cut in one piece, with the edges brought over to the front as a binding to frame the design neatly. Choose a plain, firm

▲ *The rich textures and dramatic colors of this rug, blended in undulating strips, make a welcoming focus of attention in the living room.*

fabric for the border and backing which flatters all the other fabrics. A layer of batting is added to make the rug deep and cosy and comfortable to walk on.

Making the appliquéd rug

The instructions give a finished rug size of 90cm (35½in) wide by 150cm (59in) long, but you can adapt this if you wish – although it's convenient to keep the width within that of the interfacing and batting available, to avoid joins.

Try not to choose fabrics of a widely different nature, although some, like fur fabrics, will be specially chosen for their interesting texture. Short to medium pile fur fabrics are more suitable than shaggy long pile. If you find velvet difficult to manage in layers, slip a piece of tissue paper between the layers before sewing, or rearrange the strips to avoid using them together. You can use up offcuts of fabric, but it's safest to keep the grain running in the same direction by cutting across the width from selvedge to selvedge. Choose sewing thread in a series of colors to match your fabrics – it looks better if the stitching is not too obvious. The quantities given here are approximate: you can vary them depending on what you have available, using more of one fabric than another.

A clear plastic presser foot is useful when following lines exactly; an even feed presser foot will help if you have trouble getting the thicknesses through the machine. Adjust the upper and lower thread to a slightly looser tension than usual, and adjust the satin stitch to the widest setting and a close stitch.

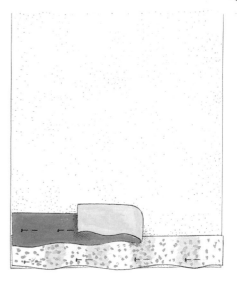

▲ *The fabrics are backed with batting for an inviting softness. You will need to choose a fairly robust fabric for the backing.*

You will need

- ◆ **46cm (½yd) each of five contrasting fabrics**
- ◆ **1.7m (1⅞yd) contrast fabric for the border and backing**
- ◆ **Matching threads**
- ◆ **3.5m (3⅞yd) mediumweight polyester batting**
- ◆ **1.6m (1¾yd) lightweight iron-on interfacing**

1 Preparing the base fabrics Trim the interfacing to measure 160 x 90cm (63 x 35½in), and cut one piece of batting to this size.

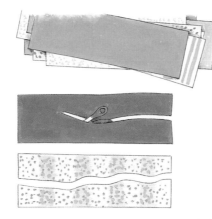

2 Cutting the strips Cut each of the fabrics in half across the width, then cut the two strips in half again, but this time cutting in an uneven, roughly undulating line, so that the strips vary in width.

3 Positioning the strips Lay the interfacing out, fusible side up. Position the first strip, right side up, with its uneven edge along one end of the interfacing. Pin another strip alongside it, with its uneven edge overlapping the straight edge of the first strip – it should overlap by at least 1cm (⅜in).

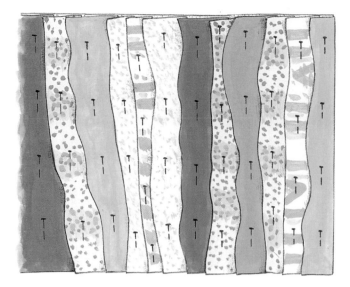

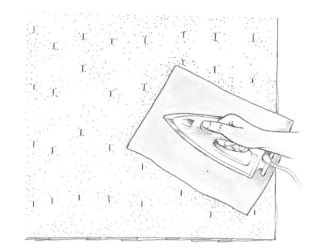

4 Arranging the design Continue placing strips over the interfacing in this way, overlapping them as you go and making adjustments for color and design – you could place some at a slight angle, for instance, and some closer together than others. The last strip should cover the end of the interfacing.

5 Fixing the design When you are satisfied with the design, turn the panel over, and fuse the pieces in place with a damp cloth and a warm iron, pressing lightly on a padded surface to avoid flattening any pile. Lay the panel right side up on the batting and tack around the edges.

6 Stitching appliqué Fit the even feed or clear plastic foot on your sewing machine. Setting the stitch length very short and the width at the widest point, work satin stitch along the first overlapping edge, using a basting thread and following the shape carefully. Repeat in this way with all the strips.

7 Trimming to size Trim the appliqué panel to measure exactly 150 x 90cm (59 x 35½in), making sure all corners are true right angles. Lay it on the remaining batting and trim this to size also. Pin and tack together around the edge.

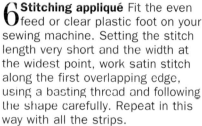

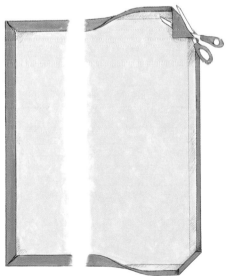

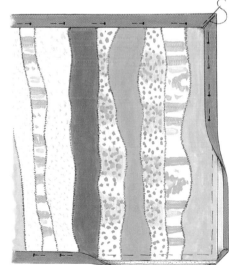

8 Cutting the backing Trim the backing fabric to measure 164 x 104cm (64⅝ x 40⅝in) – this allows a little extra for the depth of the rug. Press 1.5cm (⅝in) to the wrong side all around.

9 Mitering the corners Wrong side up, press in 5cm (2in) all around. At corners, open out the folds, then fold the corner in diagonally at the point where the folds cross, with its edges parallel to the main edges. Press, then trim 1.5cm (⅝in) from this fold. Re-fold the corner.

10 Putting the rug together Center the appliqué panel on the backing, wrong sides together, bringing side edges up to enclose the raw edges. Pin in place. Using ladder stitch, sew the edges of the miters together by hand.

11 Finishing off Using matching thread and a long straight stitch, machine the binding in place close to the fold, through all thicknesses.

Jazzy striped cushion

With the same kind of appliqué and some scraps of glamorous fabric, you can make an elegant cushion with a contemporary striped design and a neat, flat contrast border. Translucent fabrics overlaying others make an interesting layered effect, and the flat velvet border adds sophistication and impact. We used silk for the main panel, with the stripes in various shades of organza and voile, topped with crushed velvet. These instructions are for a 40cm (15¾in) cushion with a 7cm (2¾in) border.

Scraps of ritzy dress fabrics are laid over each other for depth in this design, and matched with a soft velvet surrounding frame.

You will need

- ◆ Scraps for appliqué
- ◆ 50cm (19¾in) light fusible interfacing
- ◆ 50cm (19¾in) main fabric
- ◆ 80cm (32in) velvet for back and border
- ◆ Matching threads
- ◆ 30cm (12in) zipper
- ◆ One 40cm (15¾in) inner cushion
- ◆ Paper and pencil

1 Preparing the appliqué panel *From main fabric:* cut a 45cm (17¾in) square. Fuse it to the interfacing with a warm iron and damp cloth, then trim away the rest of the interfacing.

2 Cutting the strips *From organza and voile:* cut three strips of each 45 x 8cm (17¾ x 3¼in), shaping the side edges in a randomly undulating line. *From crushed velvet:* cut three strips the same length as before, but make them slightly narrower.

3 Placing the design Space the organza strips vertically across the main panel and pin in place. Lay the voile strips on top, roughly central, then the velvet. Re-arrange to your taste – the design does not have to be symmetrical, but remember that the finished design will be 2.5cm (1in) smaller all around. Pin in place.

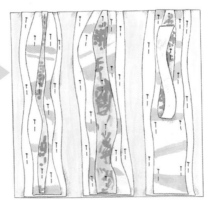

4 Stitching the design Follow the instructions in step **6** on page 27 to complete the satin stitching. Trim the panel to measure 43cm (17in).

5 Making the pattern Cut a piece of paper 54cm (21¼in) square. For the split back, fold the pattern in half, and cut two pieces, adding 1.5cm (⅝in) all around. Open pattern, and draw in the 7cm (2¾in) border and corner miters.

6 Making the border Cut out the border pieces of the pattern, discarding the center panel, pin them to the fabric, mark a 1.5cm (⅝in) seam allowance and cut out. Place two pieces right sides together and pin across one diagonal end, seam allowance as above. Backstitch at each end starting at outer edge, stopping 1.5cm (⅝in) from inner edge. Press open. Repeat to form a

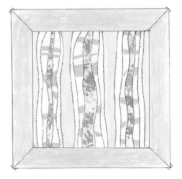

frame. Right sides together, pin inner edge of border panel to appliquéd panel. Stitch across each side, pivoting fabric around the needle at corners. Snip into seam allowances of border at each corner, just inside stitching. Open out border and press.

7 Inserting the zipper To insert the zipper in the back panel, place the two back cushion pieces right sides together and tack, 1.5cm (⅝in) in from the straight edges. Stitch 2.5cm (1in) in from each edge along tacked line. Open fabric out, wrong side up, and press seam allowances open. Center zipper right side down over seam and stitch along both tapes through all thicknesses. Remove tacking.

8 Completing the cushion Pin the back and front right sides together and stitch the outer edge; turn out and press. Pin border around the edge of the appliquéd panel through both layers, following the seamline, and topstitch. Insert cushion pad.

Pleated lampshades

*The smooth outline of a pleated lampshade adds classic
detail to a room, while the softly folded fabric gently diffuses
the light, creating a warm and welcoming glow.*

Elegant pleated lampshades make interesting alternatives to plain shades. They combine a look of classic luxury and softness without fuss or frills. Making your own is an ideal way to revamp an old lamp with the minimum of expense.

A pleated shade is quite simple to make. Only the most basic sewing skills are required – you won't need a sewing machine and you can use virtually any medium to lightweight fabric. Before choosing your fabric, pleat it in your hand, making sure that it holds the pleats without creating too much bulk. Then hold it up against a bright light – if the fabric is too fine or loosely woven, the light fitting may show through when the light is on.

With patterned fabric, the pleats will distort and hide parts of the design, but this can produce interesting effects. You can use checks, tartans and stripes as a guide to forming regular pleats.

On plain fabrics, slim, regular knife pleats look traditional; choose wider pleats to show off a pattern. Box pleats have classic elegance, while random

▲ *Pale silk, folded in box pleats around a gently sloping lampshade frame, illuminates an elegant collection of* objets d'art. *The gentle light from the lamp complements the warm candlelight.*

pleats have a more contemporary look.

The easiest shades to cover are cone and drum shapes. On drum shapes the pleats are straight, while on cone shapes they fan out towards the base. Avoid bowed, waisted or shaped-edge shades, as these are more difficult to finish well.

Making a knife-pleated lampshade

A pleated lampshade is simply a length of pleated fabric attached to the frame. You'll need to bind the frame tightly with cotton tape first – this gives a firm base on which to stitch the shade. Most fabric or craft stores sell binding tape in a range of colors. To work out the quantity you need, measure the height of all the struts and around both rings, and multiply the total by three.

You also need bias binding to finish the top and bottom edges of the shade. To work out the amount you need, measure around the top and bottom rings and add 10cm (4in) for joins.

For most lampshades, a meter (yard) of fabric is enough, but to save wastage, it's a good idea to calculate your requirements before buying. Measuring up is explained in step 2 below.

4 **Sectioning the fabric** With tailor's chalk, mark in a 3cm (1¼in) allowance on the short edges, and a 1.5cm (⅝in) allowance on the long edges. Count the spaces between the struts, and divide the fabric length within the allowances into the same number of sections. Lightly chalk vertical lines on right side of fabric to mark these sections.

You will need

- ◆ Cone-shaped lampshade frame
- ◆ Fabric
- ◆ Binding tape
- ◆ Bias binding
- ◆ Matching thread
- ◆ Tape measure and ruler
- ◆ Tailor's chalk
- ◆ Pins, needle
- ◆ Fabric adhesive

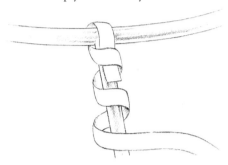

1 **Binding the frame** At the top of a strut, wrap the tape end over the top ring, then wind the tape firmly around the strut and over the loose end. Continue down the strut, winding diagonally so that each turn just overlaps the previous one. At the bottom of the strut, secure the tape end with a dab of adhesive or a few small, firm stitches. Repeat with the other struts, then bind the rings.

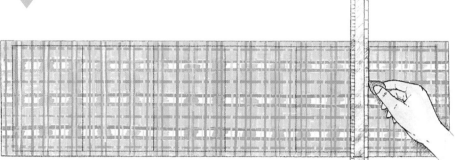

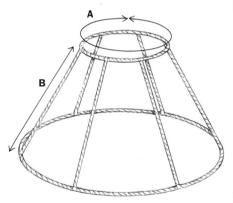

2 **Measuring up** Measure round the top ring (**A**) and multiply by three; then add 6cm (2¼in) to get the cut length of fabric. Measure the height of the frame (**B**) and add 3cm (1¼in) to get the cut width of fabric.

3 **Cutting the fabric** Cut a piece of fabric to the required length and width. If you need to add another piece to make up the required length, match the pattern carefully and add 5cm (2in) for overlaps.

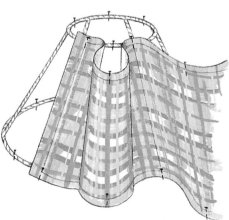

5 **Positioning the fabric** Use pins to mark the center of each fabric section along the top and bottom edges. In the same way, mark the center of each section of the frame. Right side uppermost, position the fabric on the frame with the top and bottom chalk lines on the rings. Pin the first two vertical chalk lines to the first two struts at the top and bottom.

6 **Starting the pleats** Using center points on the frame and fabric as a guide, pleat the fabric evenly between the first two struts, securing it with pins at top and bottom. The pleats will fan out at the bottom. Adjust the pleats until you are happy with their size and number. Then pin each pleat securely to the rings, with the pins at right-angles to the frame.

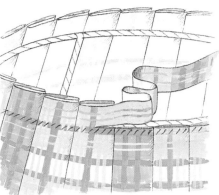

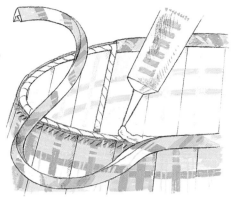

7 Continuing the pleating Working on one section at a time, continue pinning the pleats round the shade, matching them to the first section. If you need to join in extra fabric, press under a 6mm (¹⁄₄in) turning on the side edge of the new piece, slip the pressed edge into the last fold, then pin it in place. Continue pinning pleats around the frame as before.

10 Trimming the fabric Use sharp dressmaker's scissors to trim the top allowance so fabric lies level with the top of the top ring. Trim the bottom allowance in the same way.

▼ *Checked fabrics make attractive pleated shades, as the folds emphasize the color contrasts in the pattern. Self bias binding adds another interesting feature.*

11 Binding the edges Turn under 6mm (¹⁄₄in) at the end of the bias binding. Starting at a strut, apply a thin film of fabric adhesive to the top edge, and position the binding along it, over the raw edges. When you reach the start, trim the free end and turn it under so that it butts up against the first end. Bind the bottom edge of the shade in the same way.

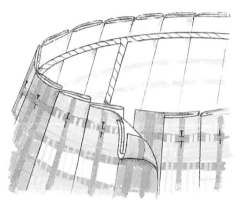

8 Finishing the end When you reach the starting point again, crease the last fold and trim off the excess fabric 3cm (1¹⁄₄in) from the fold. Pin the last fold over the first allowance.

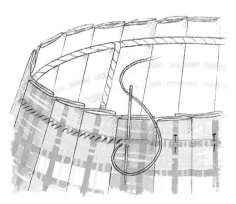

9 Stitching the pleats Working on the outside of the frame and using double sewing thread, oversew the fabric to the binding on the top ring. Repeat to oversew the fabric to the binding on the bottom ring.

Making a box-pleated lampshade

Box pleats are a sophisticated variation for a pleated shade (see the photograph on page 29). They work well on conical and drum-shaped shades. Striped fabrics can produce interesting effects – the pleats expose some parts of the pattern and hide others. You can choose broad pleats to add movement to a large frame, or smaller pleats for fine fabrics.

You will need

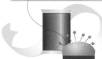

◆ **Drum or cone-shaped lampshade frame**

◆ **Fabric**

◆ **Binding tape**

◆ **Bias binding**

◆ **Matching thread**

◆ **Tape measure and ruler**

◆ **Tailor's chalk**

◆ **Pins, needle**

◆ **Fabric adhesive**

1 Preparing the frame and fabric Following steps **1-5** on page 30, cut out and position the fabric on the frame.

2 Starting the pleats Divide the top ring in the first section into equal spaces of 2.5-5cm (1-2in), and mark the spaces with tailor's chalk. Divide the bottom ring of this section into the same number of spaces and mark them. Divide the first fabric section into the same number of spaces, and pin to the chalk marks.

EASY PLEATS
Tip
If you are making lots of pleated lampshades, think about buying a pleating tool. This tool uses louvres to help you form pleats quickly and accurately. You can also use it to pleat trims such as fabric and ribbon frills. Pleating tools are sold by mail order.

▲ *Box pleats form the starting point for this pretty smocked shade. To copy this look, make a box-pleated shade and, once the shade is complete, join alternate pairs of pleats with tiny stitches. Small ribbon bows highlight the effect.*

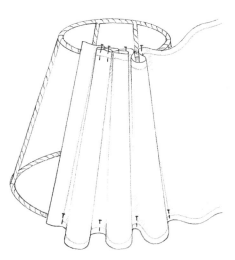

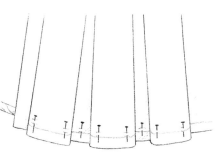

3 Forming the pleats At the top ring, form each fold of fabric into a box pleat, folding so the pleats meet at the marks. Make sure that they are equal, then pin each pleat in place.

4 Pleating the bottom Continue the pleats down to the bottom, fanning them out neatly to fit the frame as necessary. Pin the pleats securely to the lower ring, with the pins at right-angles to the frame.

5 Continuing the pleating Pleat the remaining sections in the same way, taking care to keep the pleats even and vertical. Join in extra fabric if necessary, following step **7** on page 31.

6 Finishing the shade When you reach the starting point again, finish the end as in step **8** on page 31. Then follow steps **9-11** to complete the shade.

Bowed lampshades

*For the haute couture of the lampshade world, a gently bowed
frame is covered in bias-cut fabric, eased smooth to follow the curves
and neatly lined. Make one to complement your living room.*

The shapely curves of a bowed lampshade suit any style of living room, whether traditional or contemporary. Covering your own shade means you can match your scheme exactly, and even use up scraps of fabric left over from other items. When selecting a fabric remember it will be seen on the diagonal and choose accordingly – all-over florals work fine, as do mini-prints and checks, or have fun with stripes, arranging them carefully at the seams. Plain fabrics with a surface texture, like silk Dupion or textured cotton, work well, but avoid anything too stiff or heavy. Look for light- to mediumweight fabrics which give slightly when stretched – dress cottons, satin and voile are all suitable.

Lining the shade blocks out the struts and the bulb outline when the light is on, and reflects the light, giving a brighter glow. For the lining, choose a plain lightweight fabric similar in color to the outside. Warm colors such as pink and peach create a cosy glow.

▲ *Cutting fabric on the bias adds an interesting slant to directional patterns such as checks and stripes.*

The top and bottom edges of the shade are enclosed in bias binding, which can be stuck on with fabric adhesive or slipstitched in place. We used ready-made bias binding in a contrasting color for the lampshade overleaf, but you can make your own for a more subtle look.

Making a bowed shade

Most craft stores stock bowed lampshade frames, or try mail order suppliers. The frame is first covered with binding tape to give a base on which to stitch the shade – see page 30 steps **1-2** for instructions. Quantities given here are for a 25cm (10in) diameter shade. If you are making a bigger or smaller size, for the binding tape quantity measure all the struts and around both rings and multiply by three. For the bias binding, measure around both rings and add 10cm (4in) for joins. 1m (1⅛yd) of fabric will be sufficient for the largest size.

You will need

- **25cm (10in) diameter bowed lampshade frame**
- **50cm (⅝yd) fabric**
- **50cm (⅝yd) lining**
- **Matching thread**
- **1m (1⅛yd) bias binding 2.5cm (1in) wide**
- **10m (11yd) binding tape**
- **Dressmaker's pencil**
- **Pins**
- **Needle**

▶ *Elegantly curvaceous, a bowed lampshade shows off pretty fabrics – choose a complementary binding.*

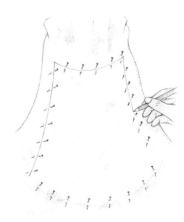

1 Preparing the frame Bind the frame with the tape, following the instructions on page 30 steps **1-2**.

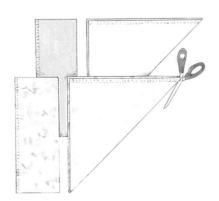

2 Cutting the fabric Fold the fabric diagonally by lining up one selvedge with the cut edge, and trim off the remainder. Repeat with the lining fabric. On the fabric only, cut along the fold to make two triangles.

3 Pinning on the fabric Wrong side out, position one triangle, point uppermost, to cover half of the frame, with 4cm (1½in) allowance all around. Starting at the center, pin the fabric to the top and bottom rings, pulling it taut and smooth. Continue down the two vertical struts.

4 Marking the shape Using the dressmaker's pencil, draw the line of the two vertical struts on the fabric, then along the pinned lines of the top and bottom rings. Unpin the fabric from the frame.

6 Making the lining Pull on each end of the fold of the lining square to stretch slightly. Center the stitched cover on the lining and cut around it. Remove the cover and stitch the lining seams, taking a 1.2cm (½in) seam. Press all seams and turn cover and lining right sides out.

9 Fitting around the gimbal Cut straight down from the top edge between the two marked lines of each gimbal to 1cm (⅜in) from the bottom, then snip out to the bottom of each line. Turn the cut edges under and re-pin the lining.

10 Stitching the lining Bring the lining fabric over the rings to cover the raw edge of the main fabric. Pin and oversew to the rings as in step **7**. Trim the lining close to the stitching.

7 Attaching the cover Fit cover on the frame, matching seams to opposite vertical struts (not gimbal struts that support the light fitting), and the marked lines to the rings. Pin the fabric to the rings, pulling taut diagonally for a smooth finish. Using double thread, on right side, oversew the fabric to the rings. Trim close to stitching.

11 Binding the edge Pin the bias binding in place to cover the raw edge of the lining, and slipstitch in place, overlapping the ends neatly.

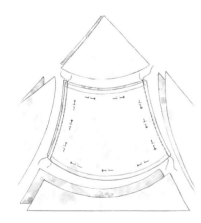

ALTERNATIVE TRIMS **Tip**
For a quicker finish, use fabric adhesive to apply a pretty matching braid to the top and bottom edges, turning in both ends and butting them closely together.

5 Stitching the seams Pin the marked triangle on its other half, right sides together. Extend the marked lines by 1.5cm (⅝in) at each end, and stitch along the lines. Trim the seam allowance to 1cm (⅜in), and the top and base edges to 1.5cm (⅝in) outside the marked lines.

8 Positioning the lining Fit the lining inside the frame, matching the seams with the cover seams and with an equal allowance at top and bottom. Draw round the gimbal struts and remove the lining.

Sixties-style shade

For a retro Sixties look, make this strikingly sculptural lampshade to light a dull corner or add interest above a table. It is very simple to make – it's just a tube of stretchy fabric with rings of various sizes sewn in at intervals.

It's important that the fabric has plenty of widthways stretch. Look for mediumweight jersey fabrics, or a novelty fabric like the one shown which has Lycra threads woven in, giving a crinkled texture. The top ring has a gimbal fitting for the bulb; the other rings are plain. Both gimbal rings and plain rings are sold in craft stores or by mail order suppliers. The shade in the picture has three rings and measures 68cm (26¾in) long, but you could add further rings to make a longer shade. Large glass beads catch the light and add interest at the bottom edge.

▶ *Fabrics woven with Lycra are perfect for this stretchy shade. Textures add shadowy effects – look for metallic or chenille fabrics for a richer look.*

You will need

- ◆ **90cm (1yd) stretch fabric**
- ◆ **Matching thread**
- ◆ **18cm (7in) diameter top ring with gimbal**
- ◆ **Two x 27cm (10¾in) diameter plain lampshade rings**
- ◆ **28cm (11in) diameter plain lampshade ring**
- ◆ **Ten large beads**
- ◆ **Dressmaker's pencil**
- ◆ **Needle**
- ◆ **Pins**

1 Cutting the fabric Decide on the width of fabric you need to stretch comfortably round the biggest ring but fit without wrinkling round the smallest; add 3cm (1¼in) for the seam. Cut a piece of fabric to this width, and trim the length to 74cm (29in).

2 Marking the ring positions On the right side, mark a line 2cm (¾in) in from the bottom and the top edges. Divide the space between into three sections, marking with lines of pins.

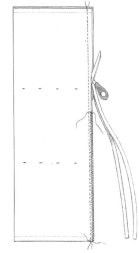

3 Stitching the seam Bring the two long edges right side together, matching all marks, and stitch, taking a 1.5cm (⅝in) seam. Use a stitch that gives with the fabric. Trim the seam allowances to 6mm (¼in) and zigzag to neaten. Turn to the right side.

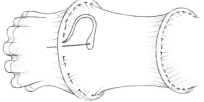

4 Stitching the inner rings Slip one of the inner rings into the tube and line it up with one of the pin lines. Pinch the fabric together around it, and pin. Using double thread, work a small stab stitch all around, close to the ring. Repeat with the second inner ring.

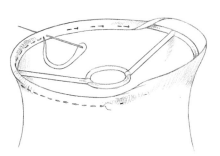

5 Stitching top and bottom rings Slip the gimbal ring inside the top edge, level with the marked line. Folding the fabric around the ring to the inside, turn the raw edge in to make a small hem. Pin and stitch with stab stitch close to the fold. Repeat for the bottom ring.

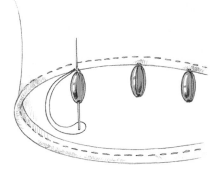

6 Adding the beads Using a thread to match the beads, sew the beads at equal intervals around the bottom ring.

Fabric screens

Practical and pretty, a fabric-covered screen is a useful addition to a living room. Use it as a chic room divider in a large room, or as an elegant way to hide unattractive clutter.

A hinged, fabric-covered screen can be a real asset in the home, serving a number of practical and decorative purposes. Today's lifestyles demand that a living room serves a series of activities – so ways of separating the different parts of our lives make for a calmer, less stressful home. This is true in even the smallest of spaces: shut off the piled-up ironing board, the home office, an untidy stack of shelving, or even a dining area after a meal, and you can forget it's there until it's time to deal with it. You can use a fabric screen to hide piles of children's toys or the TV viewing area or to shut off a hobby area. Move it to the spare bedroom to conceal piles of storage boxes when you have guests to stay, and in a studio apartment use it to make the switch from bedroom to daytime living.

With a fabric screen you have the added advantage of being able to create a strong style statement in your choice of panel shape, fabric and finish. Solid panel screens ready for you to cover are available from mail order suppliers, or you may snap up a junk-store bargain. Some screens have attractive arched or scalloped tops, and they may also vary in size – a mini-screen is ideal to block off an empty grate, or even a window.

Pick a single fabric to tone with your decor, or a series of complementary designs – cover each side in a totally different fabric, so you can turn the screen around to give the room a completely new look. For designer style, create a picture with fabric paints, or stitch on a unique appliqué feature. Edges can be finished with braid or upholstery nails, offering more design possibilities.

◀ *The gracefully scalloped top of this screen sets it perfectly in period to match the intricate detail of a striking Toile de Jouy fabric in crisp red and white.*

Covering a screen

A typical folding screen has a number of narrow panels – there may be three or four – joined with a row of hinges. Modern screens have panels of solid wood, like blockboard or MDF, while older ones may consist of an outer frame only. For both types the technique is the same, as the fabric is attached to the outer edges only.

Standard room screens may be from 150-180cm (59-71in) high, with panels about 41cm (16in) wide. Smaller ones, often termed 'firescreens', are about 89cm (35in) high, with panels 35cm (14in) wide. You need enough fabric for both sides of each panel, allowing for the panel depth plus 2.5cm (1in) all round. A layer of light- or medium-weight polyester batting or curtain interlining under the fabric gives a soft, luxurious finish. Allow enough braid or upholstery nails to go all around each panel. The braid should be no wider than the panel depth.

If revamping an old screen, you will need tools for ripping out old fabric and nails or staples.

You will need

- ◆ Hinged screen
- ◆ Furnishing fabric
- ◆ Batting or interlining
- ◆ Decorative braid or upholstery nails
- ◆ Fabric adhesive
- ◆ Dressmaker's pencil
- ◆ Hammer and tacks or staplegun and staples
- ◆ Screwdriver
- ◆ Awl

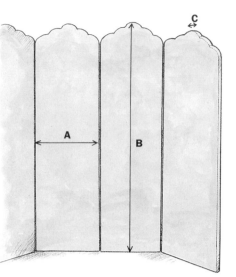

1 Measuring up To calculate fabric requirements, measure the width (**A**) and the height (**B**) of one panel, adding the depth (**C**) plus 2.5cm (1in) all around. Allow twice this amount for each panel – you should get two average panels from a width of fabric. Measure around the edges plus 10cm (4in) for braid.

2 Preparing the screen Lay the screen flat and remove the hinges using the screwdriver. If necessary, remove old fabric and fixings carefully as on page 48 steps **1-2**, and sand edges smooth.

3 Cutting the batting Lay the batting out and place one panel on top. Draw around the panel with the dressmaker's pencil, remove the panel and cut out. Using this piece as a pattern, cut two pieces of batting for each panel.

4 Attaching the batting Apply a 2.5cm (1in) line of adhesive around the first panel close to the outer edges. Press one of the batting pieces on to it, smoothing out any wrinkles. Turn the panel over and repeat for the other side. Apply batting to the rest of the panels in the same way.

5 Cutting the fabric Lay the fabric out wrong side up and place one panel on top. Draw around the panel with the dressmaker's pencil, remove the panel and add the depth of the panel plus 2.5cm (1in) all around. Using this piece as a pattern, cut out two pieces for each panel.

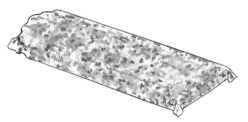

6 Positioning the back fabric Lay the first panel flat with the back facing up, and center a piece of fabric over it, right side up. Fold the fabric to the outer base edge of the panel and secure with a few tacks or staples. Pull the fabric taut at the top edge and secure in the same way.

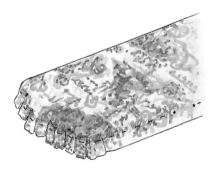

7 Securing the back Check fabric is straight, adjusting if necessary. Secure the sides at intervals, marking positions of hinge screws. Work all around the edge, tacking or stapling at 5cm (2in) intervals. At curves and corners, fold excess fabric into pleats and secure.

8 Trimming the edge With scissors, trim off the raw edges of the fabric to just within the panel depth.

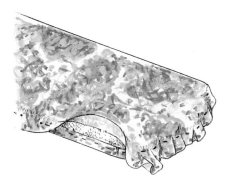

9 Covering the front Turn the panel over. Center another piece of fabric in the same way, and repeat steps **6-8**, bringing the front fabric over the edge of the back cover. Position the tacks or staples between existing ones, and transfer the hinge markings.

10 Re-aligning the hinges Lay each panel flat and lay the hinges in place on the side edges. Use an awl to pierce the fabric through the hinge at the screw positions, and remove tacks or staples in the way of the hinge.

11 Trimming with braid or nails Lay each panel flat. Apply braid or nails (as described on page 40) all around the edge, starting at the base of one side of a panel. Mark the screw positions with pins if using braid, and leave gaps for the hinges if nailing.

▲ *Simple and striking, giant blue checks give crisp, neat definition to a three-panel folding screen with an elegant curving top. Bold designs and jumbo patterns work well on the simple, flat surfaces of screens, distracting the eye from the background. A different fabric can be used on the back.*

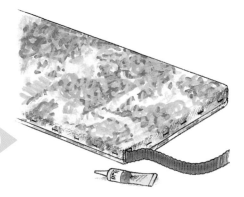

12 Re-attach the hinges Put hinges in the marked positions to complete the screen.

Tip

PINBOARD SCREEN
Turn a paneled screen into a useful pinboard with braid criss-crossed and interlaced across each panel. Staple the ends of the braid at the side edges before adding the final braid or nail trim.

Covering an open-frame screen

Period-style screens, which are sometimes constructed of open frames for each panel, can be given a fresh, up-dated look by making simple fabric panels with decorative tabs at top and bottom to loop around the frames. Using Velcro to secure the tabs means the fabric panels can easily be removed for cleaning. In these instructions, the screen panels have narrow inner rods to take the tabs, leaving the outer decorative frames free, but you can do exactly the same with a plain style frame.

Use a woven design which looks good from both sides for the screen panels. If you prefer, you could use two thinner fabrics and seam the edges right sides together before turning out. Choose a contrast fabric for the tabs, and pick another color for the buttons.

Finishing with braid

Turn under the raw edge of the braid and fix with a tack, then stick the braid back over the tack. Working on 15cm (6in) sections at a time, apply adhesive to the braid and press in place, keeping it taut. Fold the loose end under and secure temporarily with a tack until the glue has set. Remove the tack.

Using upholstery nails

Decorative nails or nail strip can be used instead of braid. Apply the nails to cover the raw edge and tacks, making sure heads butt up to one another with no gaps between. To apply nail strip, measure the length needed and position it, making sure there is a true nail as near to each end as possible. Decorative nails and nail strip are available from fabric and craft stores.

You will need

- ◆ Open frame screen
- ◆ Firmly woven furnishing fabric for panels
- ◆ Contrast fabric for tabs
- ◆ Matching threads
- ◆ Three buttons per panel
- ◆ Six Velcro spots per panel
- ◆ Needle

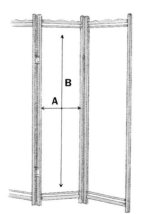

1 Measuring up Measure the width of each panel inside the frame (**A**). Measure the length from the outer edge of the frame or rods, less 5cm (2in) at each end (**B**).

2 Cutting out Add 6cm (2¼in) to **A** and **B**, and cut one piece this size for each panel. For the tabs, cut six strips per panel in contrast fabric, 12 x 19cm (4¾ x 7½in).

3 Hemming the panels On each panel, press under 1cm (⅜in) then 2cm (¾in) hem, folding at an angle at the corners for a neat miter. Stitch close to the fold.

4 Making the tabs Right sides together, fold each tab lengthways and stitch the long edges in a 1cm (⅜in) seam, leaving a 5cm (2in) center gap. Center and press seam open, then stitch the short edges in a curve. Trim and clip seams; turn out and press.

5 Positioning the tabs Spacing them equally across the width, place three tabs right side up, on the wrong side of each panel end, with the tab ends extending 1cm (⅜in) over the hem fold. Pin in place. On the right side of the panel, position the soft side of a Velcro spot at the tab positions.

6 Stitching the tabs Using thread to match the tabs, handstitch the Velcro spots in place, catching carefully through to the tabs.

7 Finishing off On the other end of the tabs, stitch the matching spots to the wrong side, and the buttons to the right side on the panel tops. Loop the tabs over the frame or rods and press closed.

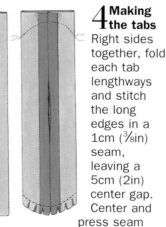
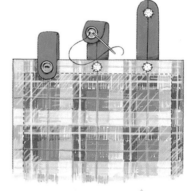
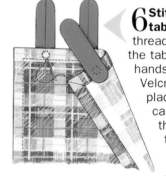

Director's chairs

*Turn old director's chairs into a matching set for the
dining room by making crisp new covers in pretty prints
or cheerful checks.*

Director's chairs are a comfortable, inexpensive and easy-to-store seating option for both indoors and out. Unfortunately, however, the plain fabric used for the seats and backs is often less than inspiring. By replacing the covers, you can give your director's chairs a new role, making them look good as extra seating at the dinner table. And you can still use them in the garden on sunny days and as casual seating around the house.

Choose a robust furnishing fabric, such as thick cotton or linen – preferably something that looks good from both sides. Bright or subtle cotton checks are always attractive; splashy floral prints soften tough linen, while thick corduroy provides a warm, welcoming touch. You can strengthen thinner fabrics with iron-on interfacing, but bear in mind that the interfacing will be visible at the back of the chair.

If you are going to use the chairs out-

▲ *Create stylish and economical seating
for your dining room by making new
covers for director's chairs. This set uses a
cheerful mix of complementary checked
and Madras fabrics.*

doors as well as in, canvas is the most practical fabric because it withstands a certain amount of damp. Buy it in bright colors or striped patterns. You could jazz up plain canvas chairs with stencilled motifs.

Covering a director's chair

The design of director's chairs varies, especially in the way the back panel is attached. Some have fixed backs with slide-on fabric panels, while others have swivel backs with fabric panels attached with fly nuts. The seat is usually tacked or stapled in place – instructions for this type are given below – but some seats slide into grooves. When removing old covers, note the fitting method and use the panels as patterns.

You may be able to make the back and seat panels from half a meter (20in) of fabric by cutting them side by side.

Fixed back chair

On a director's chair with a fixed back, the back panel has casings, which slide over two struts, along each side edge.

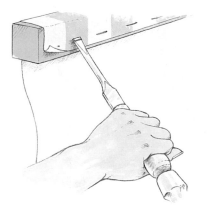

1 Removing the old covers Using a screwdriver, pry out the old tacks or staples: you may need to jam the end under the staple and hit the butt with a hammer to loosen them. Remove both the seat panel and the back panel from the frame. Try not to tear the canvas when removing it, so you can use it as a pattern.

2 Cutting the seat Making sure that any fabric design runs vertically, pin the old seat panel to the fabric, allowing 1cm (⅜in) extra for hems at the top and bottom edges and 1.5cm (⅝in) at each side edge. Cut out.

3 Cutting the back Pin old back on to fabric, adding the same hem allowances as before to top and bottom, plus enough extra on each side to make a casing (**A**) which will slip on to the struts easily. Cut out.

4 Preparing the panels If you are using furnishing fabric, apply iron-on interfacing to wrong side of panels, following manufacturer's instructions. Fit the heavy-duty sewing machine needle to your machine. Using strong sewing thread, neaten the edges of both fabric panels with zigzag stitch; alternatively, use an overlocker.

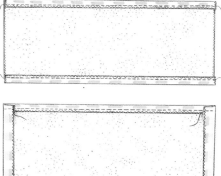

5 Finishing panels Turn under and press a 1cm (⅜in) hem at top and bottom edges of each panel; machine stitch hems in place, backstitching at ends. On seat panel, turn under 1.5cm (⅝in) on each side edge; press.

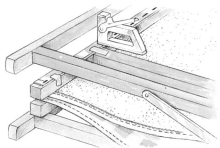

6 Fixing the seat panel Place seat across frame, centered between front and back edges. Wrap the side edges around the frame and secure with masking tape. Fold the chair and lay it on one side. Tack or staple the panel in place at the center and each end, then at 1.5cm (⅝in) intervals. Repeat for the other side.

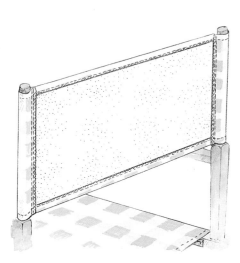

7 Completing the back panel On each side edge of the back panel, press under the allowance made for the casing. Stitch close to the edge, backstitching at the ends, then stitch another row close to the first row of stitching for added strength. Slip the casings over the back struts.

Tie-on seat pads

*Add a welcoming sense of comfort and warmth to your
dining room with a set of neatly piped and securely
tied seat cushions to soften the chairs.*

A tie-on seat pad is an excellent way to bring new color and texture into a dining room. You can even unify a collection of odd chairs by topping them all with pads of the same fabric; or you can make a tie-on cushion to soften the starkness of an occasional chair, injecting a splash of color and comfort.

The foam pad is carefully cut following a template to match the outline of the seat exactly, giving a neat, tailored effect. Trimming the cushions with piping and ties gives you a chance to add contrasting colors and patterns. You can make the ties in matching or toning fabric or use ribbons. For an elegant dining room, you can try cord ties finished with tassels to tone with the fabric, or make pretty ballerina-style ties with narrow ribbon criss-crossing down the chair legs.

▲ *Made-to-measure seat pads bring a distinct feeling of comfort to a pair of metal ribbed chairs and coordinated style to the room. The main motif is centered in the middle of each pad, while the pads are anchored to the chairs with floppy fabric ties.*

Making a tie-on seat pad

Look in your local telephone directory for a foam supplier. Foam comes in many different densities and types – your supplier can advise you on the best to use as a seat pad. A 4cm (1½in) thick, medium-density foam makes a comfortable pad. Always make sure that it is flame resistant.

1 Working out fabric amounts Measure from the front to the back of the seat. To make one cover, buy a length of furnishing fabric 10cm (4in) longer than this measurement.

2 Cutting out the template Lay a sheet of brown paper on the seat and crease round it with your fingers to get an impression of its shape. With a pencil draw over the crease, rounding off any corners. Cut out along the line and reposition on the chair to check fit. Mark position of the ties (**A**) on either side of each back strut. Take or send this template to the foam supplier to get the shape cut.

3 Marking up the fabric panels Fold the fabric, right sides together and selvedge to selvedge. Pin the template to it, just in from the selvedge and with any pattern running from front to back of the seat. Use a dressmaker's pencil to mark a 1.5cm (⅝in) seam allowance all round the template.

Tip

LAUNDERING
As the cushion is filled with a foam pad, you can put the whole thing in the washing machine without removing the cover. Make sure the fabrics you use are fully washable though – you should wash cotton furnishing fabrics before cutting out, as they may shrink by up to 10 per cent. Be sure to use pre-shrunk piping cord as well.

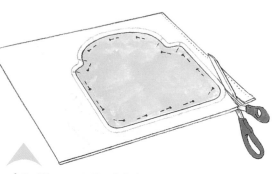

4 Cutting out the fabric panels Cut out along the marked line, through both layers of fabric. Before removing the template, mark the position of the ties on the fabric.

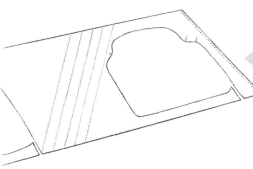

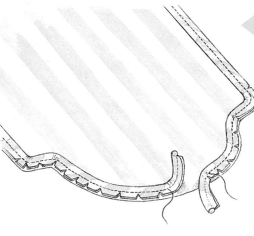

5 Cutting piping and ties From the remaining fabric, or a contrasting one, cut enough diagonal strips, 4cm (1½in) wide, for piping to go all the way around the cushion plus 10cm (4in) for joins. For the ties, cut four pieces of fabric 15 x 60cm (6 x 23½in).

6 Making and attaching the piping Center piping cord on wrong side of fabric strip. Fold strip over cord, matching raw edges. Using piping foot, machine-tack close to cord. Starting on the right side at the center back of one cushion panel, with raw edges matching, pin the piping all round the edge. Clip into the piping seam allowance to ease it round curves. Stitch in place, leaving 5cm (2in) unstitched at the beginning and end.

7 Joining the piping ends At one end, unpick the stitching to expose the piping cord and cut it off so that it butts exactly to the other end of the piping. Fold the raw end of the unpicked piping fabric under and tuck it over and around the other end neatly. Stitch this remaining section to the cushion panel through all layers.

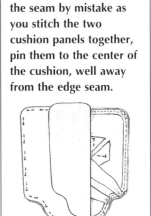

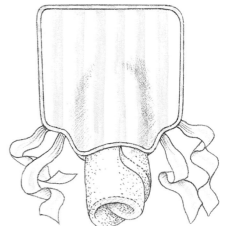

◄ *Coordinated tie-on seat pads make an important contribution to the overall decoration of the room. Here they are made in a mixture of patterns to blend with the tablecloth and harmonize an assortment of chairs.*

8 **Making the ties** With right sides together, fold each tie piece in half down its length. Cut one end of each folded tie at an angle and stitch down the long edge and across the angled end. Turn out to the right side and press.

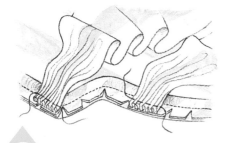

9 **Positioning the ties** On the right side with raw edges level, pin the ties in position over the piping, pleating the ends in so that they are only 2.5cm (1in) wide at the stitching line. Tack the ties firmly in place.

10 **Joining the panels** With right sides facing, pin the two cushion panels together on the piping stitching line, leaving a 15cm (6in) opening in the back for inserting the pad. Using a zipper foot, machine stitch round the cover, reversing over the ties to reinforce them. Trim seams and neaten with zigzag stitch. Turn right side out.

11 **Inserting the foam pad** Roll the foam pad up tightly before gently easing it into the cover through the back opening. Adjust its position and smooth it out. Slipstitch the opening closed. Place the cushion in position on the chair seat and tie the bows, fluffing them out for fullness.

Ballerina ties

Instead of big butterfly bows tied at the back of the chair, you may prefer the more delicate and elegant effect of these fine ballerina ties. They work particularly well on bentwood chairs with slender curving legs, where the criss-crossing ribbon emphasizes the shapely lines.

In addition to the fabric for making up the cushion, you need 3m (3⅓yd) double-sided satin ribbon, 1cm (⅜in) or 1.2cm (½in) wide, allowing 75cm (30in) for each tie. Select a color that tones in with the cover fabric.

▼ *Whether they are made in the same fabric as the seat pad, as here, or from narrow ribbons, ballerina ties are a dainty and decorative way of holding a cushion pad firmly in place on the seat.*

1 Inserting the ribbons Make up the seat cover, following the instructions for *Making a tie-on seat pad* on pages 44–45. Omit step **8**, inserting one end of each ribbon into the seam in place of the fabric ties as in step **9**. Complete steps **10** and **11**.

2 Trimming the ribbons Trim the free ends of the ribbons at an angle to prevent fraying. *Optional:* protect the ribbon ends with liquid fray preventer, available from fabric or craft stores.

3 Tying the ribbons Place the pad on the chair seat and bring each pair of ribbons around to cross at the front of the chair leg. Then take them around to the back again, keeping the ribbons flat. When you have crossed the ribbon three times on the front of the leg, finish with a little bow.

Drop-in seats

*Make new covers for worn or stained drop-in seat pads and give
your dining chairs a new lease of life. This simple upholstery project takes
very little time, and it's easy to achieve a professional finish.*

A drop-in seat pad sits inside the frame of the chair seat, and can be eased in and out without any difficulty. Most drop-in seat pads are square, although some have cut-away corners to accommodate the chair legs. To check that your dining or side chairs have drop-in seat pads, turn one of the chairs over and push gently on the underside of the seat. The seat pad should come away fairly easily.

You can make a new cover for a drop-in seat pad without sewing a single stitch. You need very little fabric, too – about 80cm (32in) square should be enough for each seat.

Select a hardwearing, mediumweight upholstery fabric; avoid very obvious checks or stripes as they can be difficult to keep straight when pulling the fabric taut. Spraying with a stain-repellent helps keep the covers fresh and clean.

▼ *Match existing chairs to a new color scheme by re-covering the seat pads; add a coat of paint to make the drabbest old chairs look fresh and new.*

Re-covering a drop-in seat pad

A seat pad upholstered in a traditional way has strips of webbing stretched across the frame; layers of hessian, hair, batting and calico, and finally the fabric cover, are stretched over the top. On the underside of the seat, curtain lining or 'bottoming cloth' conceals all raw edges and fixings.

Modern seat pads are simpler, with just a layer of foam on a plywood base. The foam layer is then covered with batting, and sometimes calico, before the fabric cover is added.

The steps given here explain how to replace the fabric cover on either a traditional or modern drop-in seat pad. If you have a traditional seat pad in poor condition, it should be taken to a specialist for re-upholstering. If the pad is made from foam, take it to a foam supplier, who will cut a new piece of foam to shape. If there is no calico lining on the pad, it is a good idea to replace the batting as well, which gives the pad a smooth finish.

Before you can put on a new cover, you need to remove the old one, by prising out the tacks or staples. For this you need an old chisel and a wooden mallet or hammer; pliers are also useful for pulling out stubborn fixings. You can use a staple gun to attach the new cover, but a hammer and tacks give you more freedom to make adjustments as you work. Before starting to work, protect your work surface with a folded blanket, and cover the blanket with an old sheet.

You will need

- ◆ **Mediumweight upholstery fabric**
- ◆ **Polyester batting**
- ◆ **Curtain lining or bottoming cloth**
- ◆ **Hammer or mallet**
- ◆ **Old chisel**
- ◆ **Pliers**
- ◆ **Small hammer and 16mm (⅝in) upholstery tacks, or staple gun and staples**
- ◆ **Stiff brush for cleaning pad**
- ◆ **Fine sandpaper**

1 Removing the fixings Push the seat pad out of the frame and turn it over. To remove tacks or staples, lodge the point of the chisel under the head of a tack or staple, and strike the end of the handle with the mallet to loosen; then prise it up and out of the pad. Use pliers to remove headless tacks or broken staples.

2 Cleaning up Remove the bottoming cloth, fabric cover and any batting. Then brush the pad free of dust. Using the sandpaper, smooth away any loose splinters.

3 Measuring up Measure the width of the seat pad from the base edge on one side, over the top and down to the base edge on the other side (**A**). Measure the depth in the same way from front to back (**B**).

4 Cutting the batting and fabric *From batting:* cut one piece **A** by **B**, and lay it centrally over the pad. *From furnishing fabric:* with the grain of the fabric running from the front to the back of the pad, and centering any motifs, cut one piece **A** plus 5cm (2in) by **B** plus 5cm (2in).

5 Starting temporary tacking Center the fabric right side up on the top of the pad. Turn the pad over, pulling the fabric to the back. In the center of the back rail, drive a tack halfway in. Repeat at 4cm (1½in) intervals on either side of the first tack, stopping 5cm (2in) from the corners.

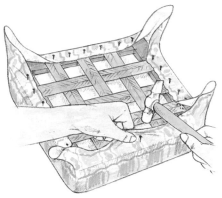

6 Completing temporary tacking With the pad on its back edge, pull the fabric tightly up to the front edge and over to the back of the pad. Temporarily tack as in step **5**. Repeat for the sides, smoothing out the fabric from the middle of the seat.

7 Mitering the corners Pull the fabric tightly over one corner to the back; tack in the center. Continue tacking towards the corner, forming pleats on either side of the corner. Trim away excess fabric from inside of pleats, fold under towards corner and tack.

Sturdy upholstery fabrics with a woven pattern are ideal for drop-in seats. They have quite a lot of 'give', so you can stretch them round the seat pad, and they wear well, too.

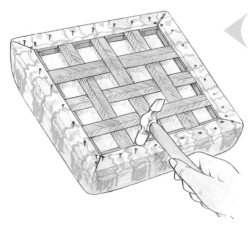

8 Finishing tacking Check the pad on the right side to make sure the fabric is as straight and taut as possible. If necessary, ease out any tacks, adjust the fabric, and tack again temporarily; check the fabric once more, then drive in all the tacks fully.

9 Finishing off Lay the pad right way up on the curtain lining or bottoming cloth and draw around it. Adding 1cm (⅜in) all around, cut out. Center the cloth on the base, turning under just enough to cover all the raw edges. Tack around to finish.

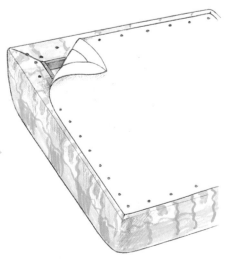

Quick seat covers

Drawstring seat covers are a quick and easy way of covering drop-in seat pads. They fit over the existing covers, so you can use them for a temporary facelift in a glitzy or unusual fabric – perhaps for a special occasion. You can also make a cheap calico set and use them to give more expensive fabric covers protection from everyday wear and tear.

Make sure you choose a lightweight fabric for the quick seat cover, or you may have difficulty fitting the seat back into the chair frame. You will also need matching sewing thread, a bodkin or large safety pin, a dressmaker's pencil, and enough narrow tape or cord to go around the seat plus an extra 20cm (8in).

1 Cutting out With fabric wrong side up, lay the pad on top. Draw around the pad with the dressmaker's pencil. Add 15cm (6in) all around and cut out.

2 Making the casing Press under 1cm (⅜in) then 2cm (¾in) all around. To miter the corners, unfold the larger hem, then fold each corner diagonally across the corner point and press. Turn in the hem neatly again. Stitch around close to the inner fold, leaving a 5cm (2in) opening at the center back.

3 Threading the cord Measure all around the cover and add an extra 20cm (8in); cut a piece of cord or tape to this length. Thread the cord or tape on to the bodkin or safety pin, then feed it through the casing, leaving the ends loose.

4 Fitting the cover Center the fabric cover over the seat pad, then pull up the cord or tape to gather the cover around the pad. Tie the ends in a bow and adjust the gathers. Then push the pad back into the chair frame.

◄ *Dress up your chairs for a special occasion with dazzling party covers pulled over the drop-in seats; or make calico ones to protect special covers from everyday wear and tear.*

Fitted tablecloth

*Perfect for the tailored, uncluttered look, a fitted
tablecloth with a 'miniskirt' is the ideal way to protect a polished
surface during the day, or dress it up for dinner at night.*

Define the lines of a round or
oval table with an elegant fitted
cloth, made in two complementary fabrics and piped at the top for
a neatly trimmed edge. A short cover like
this has a smart look for daytime, covering any signs of wear on an old table, and
it is also perfect for evening dining, since
the skirt is cut short enough not to get
in the way of your knees.

Choose a mediumweight, washable
fabric for the main part of the tablecloth. The fabric needs to be crisp and
firm enough to hold its shape. A stripe
or check works well for the hem border
as it is economical to cut it on the cross
alongside the piping; if you want to use
a directional pattern, cut the strips
straight across the fabric.

To avoid having seams across the top
of the cloth, try to choose a fabric which
is wider than the table top. If this is not
possible, you will need to join panels on
either side of a width.

▲ *Sophisticated gray linen, bordered
and piped with a crisp matching check,
makes an elegant setting for fine china
on this round table.*

Making a fitted tablecloth

These instructions are for a circular table cover with a bias cut border and piped edge. The skirt has a finished depth of 18cm (7in). To make a cloth for an oval table, make a paper pattern of the table top first.

You will need

- ◆ Furnishing fabric for top and skirt
- ◆ Contrast fabric for piping and border
- ◆ Matching thread
- ◆ Piping cord
- ◆ Tape measure
- ◆ Two self-cover buttons
- ◆ Scissors
- ◆ Dressmaker's chalk

▲ *It is best to keep the skirt length short and neat for comfort when sitting, and to allow room for the chairs to be pushed in close without crumpling the cloth.*

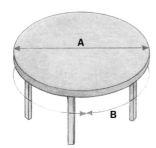

1 Measuring up Measure the diameter of the table top and add 3cm (1¼in) (**A**); measure the circumference and add 3cm (1¼in) (**B**).

2 Preparing the top fabric Cut a length of main fabric to **A**. If the fabric width is narrower than **A**, cut and join two pieces as on page 22 *Making a plain cloth,* step **2**.

3 Cutting the top fabric Fold top fabric in four. From center corner, measure and mark half of **A** plus 1.5cm (⅝in). Mark off at intervals around the quarter. Join marks in a curve; cut one layer at a time and open out.

4 Cutting the skirt *From the main fabric:* for the top half of the skirt, cut enough 15cm (6in) strips across the width to measure **B** when joined end to end. *From the contrast fabric:* for the lower half of the skirt, cut enough 15cm (6in) wide bias strips to make up a piece to measure **B** when joined together. Press the bias strips in half lengthways.

5 Piping the edge *From the contrast fabric:* for the covered piping, cut enough bias strips to measure **B** plus 7cm (2¾in). Cover the piping cord and stitch the piping to the edge of the top piece.

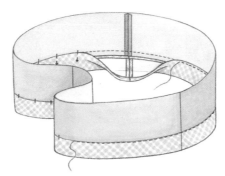

6 Seaming the skirt Right sides together, join the main fabric pieces and contrast pieces to make two long strips. Right sides together, pin and stitch one long edge of the contrast border to the bottom edge of the skirt, and press the seam towards the border.

7 Completing the skirt Check and adjust the length of the skirt to measure exactly **B**. Right sides together, pin and stitch the two short ends; press seam open. Press under 1cm (⅜in) at the raw edge of the contrast border and turn to wrong side to cover previous row of stitching on inside. Pin, then stitch in the ditch (i.e. in the groove where the fabrics meet) on the right side. Press fold.

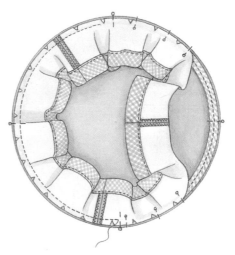

8 Attaching the skirt Fold the top of the cloth into quarters and mark at the folds; repeat with the top edge of the skirt. Right sides together and matching marks, pin the skirt to the piped edge, sandwiching the piping in between and clipping the seam allowance if necessary. Stitch; trim the seam and zigzag to neaten.

Bordered tablecloth

*A formal tablecloth with a wide border adds a
dramatic splash of color to a room. Neat miters at the
corners and a smart braid trim give a crisp finish.*

A custom-made tablecloth with a dramatic border can turn your dining table into a grand feature. You could also make an eye-catching cloth to cover an occasional table that's past its best, or a small, square cloth to top a circular cloth for a round table.

A richly textured damask or a subtle weave is ideal for the main fabric. For the border, choose a fabric that makes the most of the mitered corners – stripes and checks work well. Add impact with a braid trim in a contrast color that accentuates the sharp lines and corners.

▼ *Damask in mellow, old gold is a luxurious choice for a formal tablecloth that is purely for display. Adding a deep mitered border in russet red and ivory enriches the color theme and look of the finished cloth.*

Making an unlined, bordered tablecloth

When deciding on the drop of the tablecloth, bear in mind that the corners hang lower than the sides. If you make a floor-length cloth, for example, the corners will trail on the floor.

The border is laid over the fabric, rather than being added on around the edge. Choose the width of the border to suit the size of the cloth – this one has a 9cm (3½in) border.

To work out the fabric quantities you require, see steps 1-3 right. If the main fabric is not wide enough for the finished cloth width, buy twice the length. Depending on which way you want the pattern to run, you can cut the border strips either across the width or along the length of the fabric.

You will need

◆ **Furnishing fabric**

◆ **Fabric for border**

◆ **Braid**

◆ **Matching thread**

◆ **Dressmaker's pencil**

1 Measuring up Measure the width (**A**) and the length (**B**) of the table. Decide on the drop of the cloth (**C**) and the depth of the border (**D**).

2 Cutting the main fabric Add twice the drop **C**, plus 3cm (1¼in) for seam allowances, to both the table width **A** and length **B**. Cut a piece of main fabric to these measurements. If the fabric is not wide enough, join two equal pieces on either side of a width (see page 22 step **2**). For a neat finish, use flat-fell seams to join the widths.

4 Joining border strips Right sides together, join the border strips to make pieces long enough for each edge of the cloth, plus a little extra for pattern matching at the corners. Trim the seams to 1cm (⅜in) and press them open.

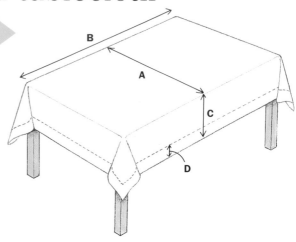

3 Cutting the border pieces Add 3cm (1¼in) to the border depth **D**, and cut enough strips to go all around the edge of the tablecloth – allow enough fabric to be able to center the pattern if necessary, or to adjust so that the pattern matches at the corners.

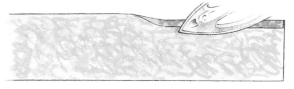

5 Preparing the borders On one long edge of each border (the top edge if there is an obvious vertical pattern), turn under 1.5cm (⅝in) and press.

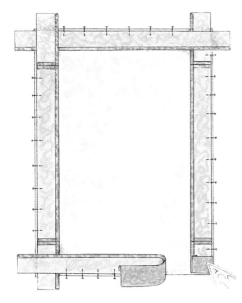

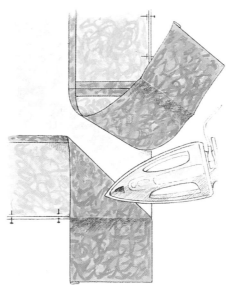

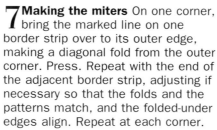

6 Applying the borders On the wrong side of the cloth, and matching raw edges, center and pin the border strips right side down along the edges of the cloth, leaving the overlapping ends at the corners free. Mark a line on each border where it crosses the main fabric edge. Fold along the line and press it with an iron.

7 Making the miters On one corner, bring the marked line on one border strip over to its outer edge, making a diagonal fold from the outer corner. Press. Repeat with the end of the adjacent border strip, adjusting if necessary so that the folds and the patterns match, and the folded-under edges align. Repeat at each corner.

8 Stitching the miters Trim off the excess fabric 1cm (⅜in) from the diagonal folds. Right sides together and matching raw edges and fold lines, pin and tack the two strips together. Lay them flat on the cloth again to check the miter, then stitch along the tacking line. Press seams open. Repeat at each corner.

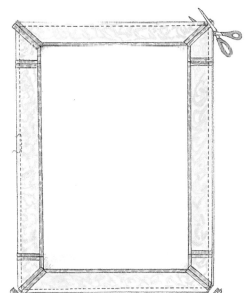

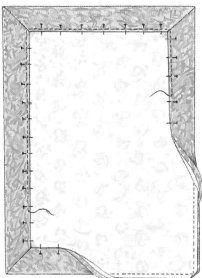

▲ *Be guided by the proportion of the border when selecting the best width of braid – it should be wide enough to show up well from a distance, without dominating the border.*

9 Stitching the outer edge Stitch all around the outer edge of the cloth and border, taking a 1.5cm (⅝in) seam allowance and pivoting at the corners. Trim the seam to 1cm (⅜in). Clip across the corners close to the stitching. Snip into the seam allowances of the miters on the border, close to each mitered corner.

10 Stitching the inner edge Turn the border to the right side of the cloth and press, making sure the seam lies exactly on the edge of the cloth. Pin in place. Secure the border by topstitching close to the inner edge all around.

Adding a braid trim

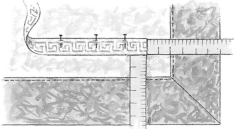

1 Applying the braid Decide where to place the braid on the main fabric. Beginning at one corner, pin the braid along one side, carefully measuring the distance from the border and taking care not to stretch the braid.

2 Turning the corner At the next corner, turn the braid back on itself and crease; fold back again at right angles, with the outer edge along the fold. Pin. Continue in this way through the other two corners.

3 Making the last corner Lap the end of the braid over the first end. Turn the overlapping end under, folding it diagonally so that it forms a miter at the corner. Trim excess to 1cm (⅜in) from outer edge of braid.

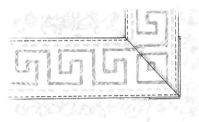

4 Completing the trim Tuck the 1cm (⅜in) allowance under the first end. Stitch all around the outer edge of the braid, close to the edge; repeat at the inner edge.

Making a lined, bordered tablecloth

Adding a lining to the cloth means that you do not need to use flat-fell seams to join widths, as all the raw edges are enclosed. It also gives the cloth extra thickness. It's best to use a colorful toning or contrast fabric, as the lining comes to the very edge of the cloth. A substantial tablecloth like this could double up as a throw on a sofa. Buy the same amount of lining as main fabric.

You will need

- ◆ Furnishing fabric
- ◆ Contrast fabric for lining
- ◆ Fabric for border
- ◆ Braid (optional)
- ◆ Matching thread
- ◆ Dressmaker's pencil

▼ *Use this method to make a cloth of any size – just relate the width of the border to the scale of the cloth. A large, light cloth, such as this, benefits from being lined.*

1 Measuring up and cutting out Cut out the lining in the same way as the main fabric, following steps **1-3** on page 54. Then cut out and stitch the border pieces together following steps **4-5**.

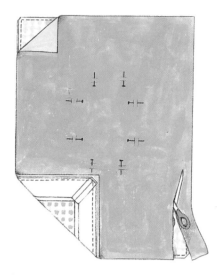

3 Adding the top layer Before turning the border right side out, lay the main fabric, right side up, on the wrong side of the lining, and smooth out. Pin together around the center area. Trim off the finished width of the border **D** less 1cm (³⁄₈in), all around the main fabric piece.

2 Adding the border Following steps **6-7** on page 54, position and stitch the border to the *right side* of the lining only, instead of the wrong side of the main fabric.

4 Completing the cloth Tack round the edge of the main fabric. Turn the border to the right side, over the edges of the main fabric. Pin and then stitch close to the folded inner edge of the border, through all the layers. If you wish, you can add the optional braid, as described on page 55.

Stiffened fabric bows

*Give table linen, plant pots or even baskets a new lease
of life with stiffened fabric bows. Use them to coordinate your
dining room decor and create a glamorous display.*

Stiffening fabric with a solution of glue before making it into bows gives bow trims a professional finish – and you can assemble sturdy bows without sewing a single stitch.

You can use stiffened fabric bows to decorate a whole range of accessories for your dining room. Add a simple, single bow to the top of a picture or mirror frame, for example, or make one with long, flowing tails to embellish a plain wicker tray or basket, or a set to decorate your table for a special occasion. Single or double bows, with or without tails, also make pretty finishing touches for a set of mismatched flower pots disguised with coordinated fabric wrappings.

The bows are easy to make from two or more pieces of fabric, which are soaked in a solution of PVA adhesive, shaped into a bow, then left to set. As the PVA dries, the fabric hardens, setting the bow

▲ *Create a set of pretty, bow-trimmed plant containers from a selection of flower pots. They are wrapped in fabric and trimmed with bows – the covering and bows are both stiffened with adhesive.*

permanently in shape. You need to leave the fabric to dry overnight or longer, depending on the size of the bow and the weather conditions. When dry, the stiffened bow has the texture of pottery.

Making stiffened bows

The steps below explain how to make a single bow without tails. Cut two pieces of fabric – one for the main part of the bow (the loop) and one for the knot. For a more dramatic effect, you can add flowing tails or make a lavish double bow; see page 59 for instructions.

PVA adhesive, which is used to stiffen the fabric, is available from art stores.

You will need

- ◆ Light to mediumweight cotton fabric
- ◆ PVA adhesive
- ◆ Old mixing bowl and spoon
- ◆ Rubber gloves
- ◆ Wire
- ◆ Pins
- ◆ Foil

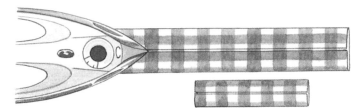

1 Cutting out Decide on the finished width and depth of the bow. *For the loop:* cut a strip of fabric twice the required bow width plus 1.2cm (½in), by twice bow depth plus 6mm (¼in). *For the knot:* cut a shorter strip of fabric, half the finished depth of the loop. Press long edges of each piece to wrong side, to meet at the center.

2 Mixing the stiffening solution Wearing rubber gloves and using a spoon, mix one part PVA to four parts of water in the bowl; stir well. Soak the strips in the PVA solution and smooth off excess.

3 Forming the bow Fold the loop strip so the short ends overlap slightly at the back. Pinch the loop together at the center and wrap a piece of wire around to gather up the fabric. Twist ends of wire together at the back to secure; trim the ends.

4 Finishing the bow Wrap the knot strip round the center, covering the wire; overlap the ends at the back and trim them if necessary. Secure the knot with pins. Ease the loops into shape and push scrunched-up foil into them to hold them in shape.

◀ For understated embellishment, make a small, single bow without tails to decorate a plain container. The smart blue and white checked fabric used for the bow on this basket would look at home in any room in the house.

5 Completing the bow Leave the bow to dry overnight in a warm room. When dry, remove the foil and stick the bow securely in place with undiluted PVA; leave to dry again. If necessary, hold the bow in place with pins while the glue sets.

▼ A textured fabric creates an interesting effect when stiffened. Here, a simple, pin-tucked fabric has been cleverly used to form a striking diagonal pattern across the bow.

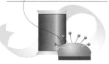

Making a bow with tails

Adding tails Make the bow as described on page 58, but cut an extra strip of fabric the required length of the tails by twice the width; press and stiffen strip as in steps **1-2**. When forming the bow in step **3**, center the loop on top of the tail strip, then continue as before. Trim the ends of the tails diagonally to prevent them fraying.

Making a double bow

Adding an extra loop Follow the instructions on page 58 to make the bow, but cut an extra loop the same depth as the first and about 4-6cm (1½-2¼in) narrower across the width. When forming the bow shape in step **3**, fold both strips in the same way and center the smaller loop on top of the larger one. Continue as before.

▲ *Add a touch of romance to a special dinner party by dressing the sides and center of the table with voluptuous bows, like these double bows with tails. Before leaving the bows to dry, arrange one to lie flat for the centerpiece. On a round table, place a bow between each seat; for a square table, put one at each corner.*

◀ *For a neat finish, trim the ends of the tails diagonally, as here, or cut them to form an attractive, inverted V-shape.*

Fabric-wrapped pots

Disguise flower pots by wrapping them in fabric to coordinate with your room. You can use new pots or recycle old ones; simply wash and dry them before use and rub down any rough edges of terra-cotta pots with sandpaper.

Closely woven fabrics are ideal; avoid large prints, unless the pot is very big. Small prints, such as florals and polka dots, suit any size of pot; take care with stripes and checks, as the pattern can distort over the shape of the pot.

You will need

All materials as for the bow on page 58, plus:

◆ **Flower pot**

◆ **Sandpaper**

◆ **Pencil, ruler and paper**

◆ **Paint brush**

◆ **Scrap of felt**

◆ **Varnish or fabric protector**

▼ *For a striking display, use stiffened fabric to cover an old flower pot that's seen better days – a single bow adds a pretty touch. A combination of bold, vibrant colors or pretty cotton mini prints and checks will catch the eye.*

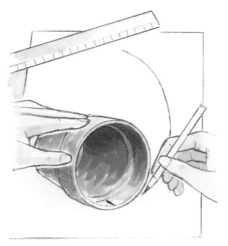

1 Drawing the paper pattern Mark a vertical line inside the flower pot, at right angles to the rim. Lay the pot on the paper. Starting at the marked line, roll the pot sideways, drawing a line to follow the curve of the rim until you reach the mark again. Roll it back along the curve, this time drawing a line to follow the base edge.

2 Cutting the pattern Draw straight lines with a ruler at each end to join the curved lines; mark the center of the pattern. Cut out, allowing 5cm (2in) for turnings at the top and base and 1.2cm (½in) at one side edge.

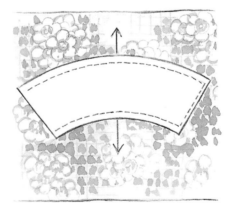

3 Cutting out the fabric Wrap the pattern around the pot to check the shape and size; adjust the pattern if necessary. Then place the pattern on the right side of the fabric, with the center on the straight grain; cut out.

4 Sealing the pot Using the spoon and bowl, mix one part PVA and five parts water and stir well. Paint the PVA solution on the inside and outside of the pot and leave to dry. This seals the surface and helps the fabric to stick.

5 Wrapping the pot Mix one part PVA with four parts of water, stirring well. Immerse the fabric in the solution and smooth off the excess. Wrap the fabric round the pot, smoothing it over the sides of the pot and making sure it fits closely under the rim.

6 Finishing off Cut the top and base overlaps into small strips. Working with alternate strips and adding more glue as needed, smooth in place. Cut a circle of fabric or felt a little smaller than base of pot; glue to base. Leave to dry overnight. If you like, spray pot with fabric protector or seal with clear varnish; leave to dry.

Tip

SEALING A WRAPPED POT

Sealing your finished pot gives extra protection from dirt and water spills. Varnish gives a waterproof finish but yellows fabric slightly. For white and bright colors, use a spray-on fabric guard suitable for soft furnishings. It's not waterproof, but gives adequate protection.

Wired ribbon

Shimmering wired ribbon is a decorator's dream.
Bows and roses are made in an instant and look
magnificent in a variety of dining-room styles.

Wired ribbon has fine-gauge wire woven along both edges. The wire is invisible and so fine that you can easily cut through it with scissors. The advantage of using wired ribbon over ordinary ribbon is that it is easily molded into full-bodied shapes and retains the shaping well.

There are lots of appealing ways you can use wired ribbon in the dining room. Make bows to trim lampshades, baskets and cushions; or use them to embellish window treatments, as shown above. You could tie them around candlesticks for an unusual table decoration.

A dining table decked out with well-chosen table linen, crockery, cutlery and pretty extras, such as flowers and candles, is a breathtaking sight. For special occasions, napkin holders made with wired-ribbon bows and roses add essential color and style to your table.

▲ *Wired ribbons are useful for creating highly decorative effects virtually instantaneously. Here, two lengths of wired ribbon are tied off in two full, stiff bows and act as slings for hitching up a plain bundle blind.*

Bow and rose napkin holders

To make a rose, hold the end of the wire along one edge, having secured the other end, and push the ribbon into gathers. Trim the excess wire, leaving a little to bend back. Wind into a rose shape and secure with a few stitches through the base.

You will need

For four napkin holders:

◆ 2.8m (3yd) of 4cm (1½in) wide wired ribbon
◆ 60cm (⅔yd) of 6mm (¼in) wide elastic
◆ Matching thread
◆ Tape measure
◆ Scissors
◆ Pencil

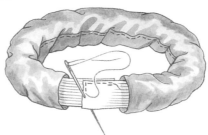

1 Making the elasticated ring Cut a 14cm (5½in) length of elastic and a 20cm (8in) length of wired ribbon. To stitch the ribbon into a tube, roll it around the pencil and work running stitch from one end of the tube to the other. Thread the elastic through the tube and stitch the ends together. Turn in one end of the ribbon and slipstitch it to the other end.

▼ *To make a rose napkin holder, make a rose using 50cm (19¾in) of ribbon and stitch it on to the ring over the join.*

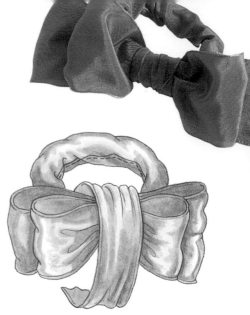

2 Adding a ribbon bow Cut a 50cm (19¾in) length of wired ribbon. Fold it so that there are two loops either side and the raw ends lie over what will be the center of the bow. One of these should be a 10cm (4in) tail of ribbon at the back of the bow. Place the bow on the napkin ring and wrap the tail around the ring. Stitch the ends of the ribbon to the inside of the ring.

Blackwork table linen

*This smart table mat and napkin set is worked
in just one stitch – backstitch – and requires only one
color of embroidery floss.*

B lackwork is a fascinating style of embroidery which is traditionally worked using thread in just one color – black. It's very free form – you can use practically any stitches you like and you can even use different colors. The only rules are that you should work the stitches in a stabbing motion and use an evenweave fabric.

The style was first popularized in England by Catherine of Aragon, the first of Henry VIII's six wives – indeed, the technique is often called Spanish Blackwork after her. Originally it was used to decorate clothing, particularly cuffs, sleeves, collars and nightwear. It was worked in black silk thread on white linen, and sometimes gold thread was added to brighten it up.

Blackwork is such an attractive style of embroidery that it's now used not only for clothing but also for a host of

▲ *This fine table linen set is worked entirely in backstitch using black thread, so it's very simple to make. The classic color combination ensures that it fits beautifully into any room scheme.*

other items – furnishings, linen and wall hangings. The table mat and napkins shown here are just examples of what you can do; you could apply the designs to other projects.

Blackwork table set

The table mat and napkins are designed in a series of small repeat patterns which make them remarkably easy to stitch. There are four different blocks of patterns on the mat, plus the decorative border. Pick any one of the blocks to work on the coordinating napkin. If you are making several napkins, you may like to work a different block design on each one.

You don't have to work the blackwork table linen in black. Use red

or green for a festive feel, or select whatever color suits your decor. You can even work each block on the table mat in a different color, if you wish, then copy one block in the same color on to each napkin.

Follow the charts to work the designs on the table mat and napkin. Use backstitch over two threads, except on design block 3 where some stitches are longer. Each square on the chart represents two threads.

You will need

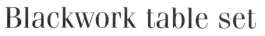

- ◆ 51 x 41cm (20 x 16in) rectangle of Zweigart 28-count Annabelle in antique white for each table mat

- ◆ 48cm (19in) square of Zweigart 28-count Annabelle in antique white for each napkin

- ◆ Embroidery frame (optional)

- ◆ Tape measure or long ruler

- ◆ Two skeins of black stranded embroidery floss (DMC 310) for each set

- ◆ Tapestry needle, size 25

- ◆ Ivory sewing thread

- ◆ Tacking thread

- ◆ Sewing needle

- ◆ Pins

Making the table mat

◀ *Work the elegant border first, followed by the four design blocks.*

Special materials

Fabrics Use any evenweave fabric as long as it isn't loosely woven; Hardanger, Aida and evenweave linen are all suitable.

Threads The type of thread and the number of strands that you use in the needle depends on the type of fabric. Ideally the thread should match the thickness of the fabric threads, although variations can create interesting tonal differences.

Needles A tapestry (blunt) needle is best in most cases to ensure you don't split the fabric threads.

1 Preparing the fabric Work machine zigzag around edge of linen rectangle. Fold fabric in half lengthways and widthways to find center. Tack along foldlines, starting from the center and making sure to follow lines of fabric threads. Mount in an embroidery frame, if you wish.

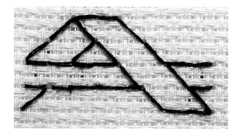

2 Working the border Begin border at center-top edge, with inner edge 130 threads from mat center (where tacking lines cross). Using one strand of embroidery floss, following chart opposite and using above sample of repeat pattern as your reference, work backstitch over two threads to stitch the border. Each square on the chart represents two threads (one stitch).

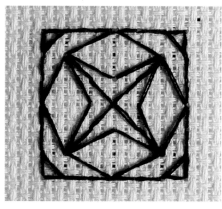

3 Working the first block design Work design block 3 on center-left of the mat first. It is based on a grid of 16 squares, each six stitches by six stitches. Start with the outline of the squares, beginning at the center horizontal line (which matches your tacking line). Use backstitch and work each stitch over two threads. When you have completed the grid, fill in each square, working from the center outwards and following the chart. Notice that the large diamonds are worked in longer stitches.

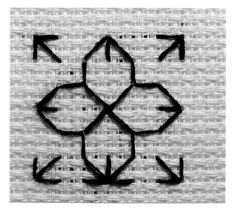

4 Working the second block Move on to design block 2. Begin four threads above the block you have just stitched. The block is based on the same-size pattern repeat as design block 3. Either work it section by section, as in the sample above, or work it systematically in rows – it's up to you.

Table mat chart

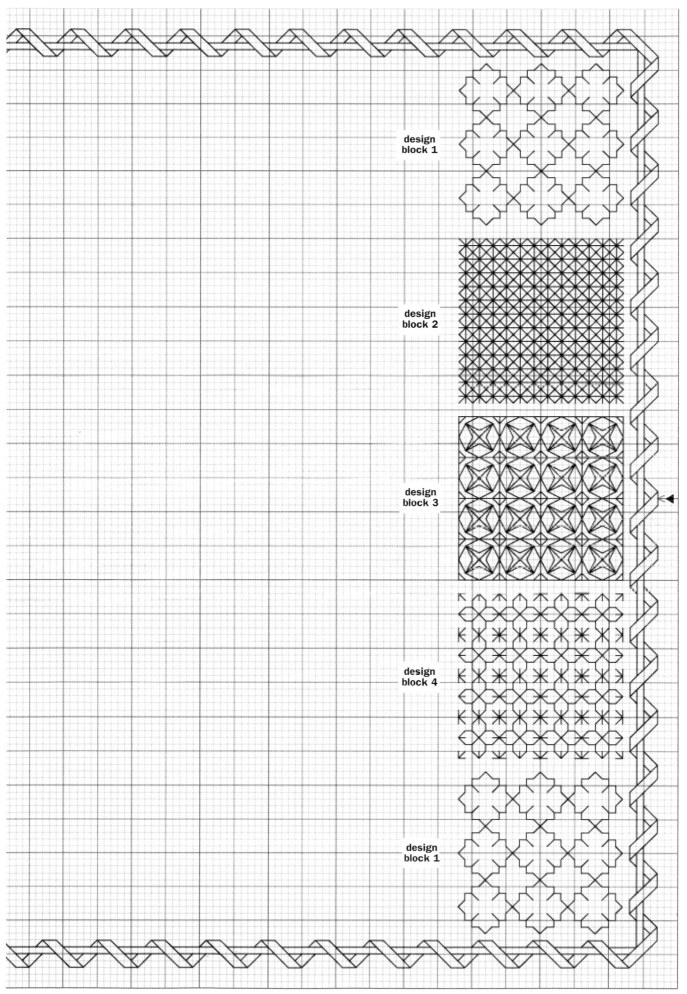

design block 1

design block 2

design block 3

design block 4

design block 1

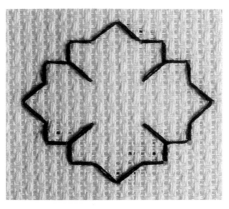

7 Finishing the blackwork Stitch the pattern blocks on the right-hand side of the mat in the same way. Notice that blocks **2** and **4** have swapped places.

8 Preparing the hem To ensure the edges are 'square', withdraw a thread 3cm (1¼in) and 4.5cm (1¾in) outside the embroidered border on each edge. Trim fabric by cutting along the outer drawn-thread line.

5 Working the third block Work design block **4** with the top edge four threads below design block **3**. This is the easiest block of all. It is made of 144 'stars', each with eight stitches radiating from the center. Work the stars one by one, starting at the center of each. Take each stitch over two strands of thread.

6 Working the fourth block Now move on to design block **1**, four threads above design block **2**. Work it section by section in backstitch over two threads, as in the sample above and following the chart. Repeat in the bottom corner, four threads below design block **4**.

9 Hemming the mat Fold fabric to the wrong side along the drawn-thread line on each edge. Fold it again to make a double hem, mitering corners as described on page 74, steps **3-4**. Pin, press, then slipstitch with ivory thread. Remove pins and press finished mat.

Making the napkin

Prepare the fabric for the napkin in the same way as the mat, following *Making the table mat*, step **1** on page 64. Work the border in backstitch over two strands of thread, positioning the inner edge 170 threads from the center, following step **2**. Work one of the block designs in a corner of the border. Hem the finished napkin in the same way as the mat, following steps **8** and **9**.

Napkin chart

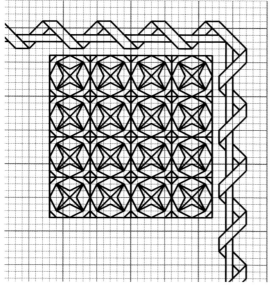

▲ *Work the same block design for all napkins or use a different pattern for each one.*

THREAD ENDS **Tip**
Start each block with a backstitch which will be worked over. To finish, darn the thread behind other stitches. Avoid long stitches as they will show through the fabric as a shadow.

Harvest festival

*The produce of the fields and orchards are the inspiration
for fabrics for your home. Fruit and vegetables bring luscious design
and a kaleidoscope of color to the kitchen.*

Fabrics glowing with the goodness of apples, pineapples, carrots and even cabbages mean you can have a wholesome-looking kitchen without going near a grocery store. The variety of styles, from bold splashes of color to subtly delicate patterns, is as great as nature's bounty. For a dew-fresh design, choose a fabric stamped with the juicy colors of exotic fruit. If your taste is more understated, look for botanical prints of celery and leeks or dainty trails of leaves and fruit that look like Victorian watercolors.

The practise of using food as decoration is a long one – ancient civilizations molded and painted swags of fruit and nuts on walls, and botanical studies of halved onions or peaches were popular in the 18th century.

Fabrics scattered with delicious produce make an obvious choice to enliven a kitchen. Many are created with this aim in mind: crisp, easily laundered cottons with fun prints work well for simple roller or Roman blinds, while smaller, tightly packed miniprints bursting with fruit are ideal for kitchen accessories like pot holders and tea cosies. But there's no need to confine fruity fabrics to the kitchen – you can enjoy them all over the house. Bring warmth to the bedroom with the lush tones of plums and cherries, or stir up the living room by covering a chair in a print of leeks or mangoes.

For upholstery, you'll find rich-textured tapestry and chenille fabrics, faithfully reproducing the shine of apples or the silky bloom of a peach. These are the perfect choice for a dining table cover or a curvy armchair. For windows, there are even diaphanous voiles shimmering with lemons and limes to give a sunny aspect in the dullest of rooms.

◀ *Cabbages, radishes and peas are among the vegetables bringing rich color and ornamentation to a cool modern kitchen.*

Mixed fruit

Fruity designs and cheery vegetable prints can easily be combined with other fabrics, particularly prints and stripes – the crisp lines have a no-nonsense, practical air that contrasts pleasingly with the flowing curves of natural forms.

Try teaming a print of vegetables with a green and white gingham for a border round a blind or piping on squab cushions; a yellow and white ticking would make a good lining for curtains printed with citrus fruit. Most traditional fruity prints will sit easily beside floral fabrics, if you aim for the same color range.

▶ *A small tablecloth printed with luscious strawberries and green leaves makes a perfect setting for a healthy meal. The fresh colors are enhanced by a crisp red and white check undercloth.*

▲ *Botanical studies of apples and pears provide interest and detail for a colorful fabric, ideal for a decorative tablecloth.*

Fifties chic

The 'contemporary' look of the Fifties featured loosely drawn, quirky fruit and vegetable designs. Their offbeat olive greens, burnt orange and spiky black colorings, or splashy primary reds and yellows, look very in tune with today's interiors. Cretonne was a common fabric for the prints in those days, but today they are often interpreted on fresh cottons or linens. Look for purple aubergines or lemon and orange designs to inspire an unusual color scheme.

▲ *Carrots and leeks sprout legs and arms in a print used for a café curtain. A deep border links the blind to the tablecloth below.*

Café curtain

This delicate linen café curtain is embellished with six rows of drawn-thread work embroidery. Bands of horizontal threads are pulled out of the fabric and the remaining vertical threads are grouped in decorative clusters.

Traditionally worked in white threads on white linen, drawn-thread work was originally used to secure hems attractively on household linens. But today bands of the stitches are often worked purely as surface decoration.

To make drawn-thread work, you withdraw (pull out) horizontal threads from the ground fabric. Then you group the remaining vertical threads into clusters with decorative stitches.

On this kitchen café curtain, ladder hemstitch is worked to secure the hemfold. However, the other hemstitches could be worked in the same way to make a decorative finish. The front of single, ladder and trellis hemstitches looks different from the back – the stitching is smaller and neater on the back, larger and bolder on the front. Use either side as the right side, depending on your preference. In this project, all the stitches, with the exception of Italian hemstitch, are worked from the wrong side of the fabric.

Work drawn-thread work on even-weave linen, selecting a fabric with threads that are easy to pull out, but closely woven enough for the fabric to

▲ *The technique of drawn-thread work is especially suited to curtains, as the clusters of threads are seen to best advantage against a window, with the light filtering through the decorative embroidered bands.*

hold its shape. Choose 28 or 32 count linen fabrics. You can stitch with either two or three strands of floss, using a blunt-ended tapestry needle for the stitching, as this slides easily between the fabric threads without catching on the material.

Making the curtain

Although traditional drawn-thread work used white embroidery floss on white fabric, there is nothing to stop you using a colored fabric or embroidery floss or both.

Experiment by stitching up a few samples using different combinations of color. Subtle pastels work best – hold the fabric up to the light when you are considering the color, as this is how you will see the café curtain when it is hanging at the window. For the stitching, use three strands of embroidery floss throughout in the size 24 tapestry needle.

Measuring up

Measure the width of the window and the required depth of the curtain. The fabric width is 1½ times the window width plus 4cm (1½in) at each side for the side hems. The fabric depth is the finished depth of the curtain, plus 1.5cm (⅝in) for the top turning and 6cm (2¼in) for the bottom hem.

Do not try to join drawn-thread work panels. If you have a very wide window, make enough separate panels to cover the width of the window and hang them together side by side on the rod.

Turning side hems

Neaten the fabric edges by pulling away any loose threads. Press the fabric with a hot steam iron and allow to dry. Turn, pin and tack a double 2cm (¾in) hem along each side edge of the fabric.

You will need

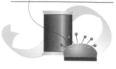

- ◆ **Zweigart 28 count Cashel linen in white, color 100**
- ◆ **DMC floss in white, three skeins**
- ◆ **Narrow curtain heading tape – the width of finished curtain plus 5cm (2in)**
- ◆ **Tapestry needles, size 22 and 24**
- ◆ **Tacking thread and sewing needle**
- ◆ **White sewing cotton**
- ◆ **Small, sharp scissors**
- ◆ **Pins**
- ◆ **Curtain hooks and rings**

Withdrawing threads for the hem band

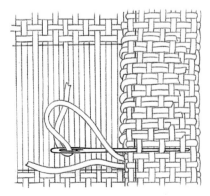

1 Marking band Mark band across fabric with two horizontal rows of tacking, making sure tacking stitches fall between two horizontal fabric threads. Position lower edge of band 11cm (4¼in) up from raw edge and make it 12 threads deep. Mark center of band with a vertical row of tacking.

2 Cutting the threads Using a small, sharp pair of embroidery scissors, carefully cut 12 horizontal fabric threads at the center of the band.

3 Drawing out the threads Using the size 22 tapestry needle to draw out the fabric threads, withdraw the cut threads up to the edge of the side hems, making sure you leave a number of vertical threads which divides exactly by four.

4 Securing the threads At each side hem, thread the cut fabric threads individually on to a tapestry needle and darn each one back into the wrong side of the hem. Cut off the thread ends close to the fabric.

Withdrawing threads for the remaining bands

Using the size 22 tapestry needle and working as described on this page, prepare the remaining bands by withdrawing threads, working up from the hem in the following sequence:
- ◆ Leave 3cm (1¼in) of fabric intact above the hem band.
- ◆ Withdraw 12 threads for trellis hemstitch.
- ◆ Leave 1.5cm (⅝in) of fabric intact.
- ◆ For the central bands, withdraw 12 threads, leave six threads intact, then withdraw another 12 threads.
- ◆ Leave 1.5cm (⅝in) of fabric intact.
- ◆ Withdraw 12 threads for trellis hemstitch.
- ◆ Leave 3cm (1¼in) of fabric intact.
- ◆ Withdraw 12 threads for ladder hemstitch.

Working ladder hemstitch

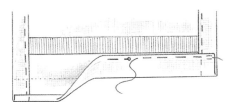

1 Turning up the hem Fold under 1cm (⅜in) along the bottom raw edge of the fabric and press. Fold under a further 5cm (2in) and press. Bring the first fold up so it meets the lower edge of the first withdrawn band, pin and tack in place.

2 Starting single hemstitch Work single hemstitch along the lower edge of the band to secure the hem as follows. Working from the wrong side of the fabric, and left to right, secure the thread end inside the fold of the hem with a tiny knot. Make a small vertical stitch to anchor the thread, catching in the top of the hemfold. Pass the needle from right to left under four of the vertical strands and pull the needle through to form the threads into a cluster.

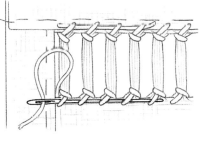

▶ *Ladder and trellis hemstitch are worked in alternate rows, with a band of decorative Italian hemstitch between the two middle rows. The threads are cut to the edge of the side hems only, in order to make a neat edge.*

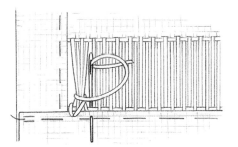

3 Working the first row Make a small vertical stitch under two horizontal threads to the right of the cluster, making sure that the point of the needle emerges through the hemfold. Continue working in this way across the band, keeping the small vertical stitches even. At the end of the band, secure the thread end under the hemfold on the wrong side and cut off the thread end.

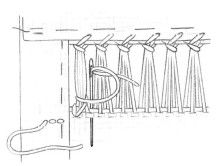

4 Working the second row Turn the fabric. Leave a tail of about 10cm (4in) and work several running stitches up to the left-hand edge of the band and begin hemstitching from left to right. Take a small vertical stitch to anchor the thread, then pass the needle under four of the vertical strands. Pull the needle through to form the threads into a cluster. Make a small vertical stitch under two horizontal threads to the right of the cluster. Continue working in this way across the band, keeping the small vertical stitches even and catching the same fabric threads into each cluster as before to make a ladder pattern.

5 Finishing off thread ends At the end of the band, secure the thread end under several stitches on the wrong side of the fabric and cut off the end. Pull out the running stitches at the other end of the band and secure in the same way.

6 Working the top band Work ladder stitch along the top band of withdrawn threads by repeating steps **4** and **5** along both top and bottom edges of the band.

Working the two trellis hemstitch bands

Trellis hemstitch is a variation of single hemstitch, worked on upper and lower ends of the vertical threads. This stitch can be worked next to a hem or as a center band. The stitches at the top and bottom of the band of drawn threads group different batches of threads together, creating a zigzag pattern.

1 Working first row Following *Working ladder hemstitch* steps **2-3** on page 71, work a row of single hemstitch from left to right along the lower edge of the threads, grouping the threads into clusters of four.

2 Working second row Turn the fabric and repeat along the remaining edge, taking two vertical threads only in the first stitch and four thereafter to form a zigzag pattern.

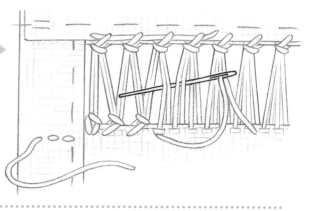

Working the wide central band

1 Working top and bottom of the central band Embroider the outside edges of the two remaining bands with a row of single hemstitch, grouping the threads into clusters of four. Turn the fabric over so the right side is facing you.

2 Working Italian hemstitch Secure the thread neatly at the right-hand end of the central intact band of six threads by working a few stitches into the edge of the side hem. Working from right to left, and grouping the threads at the top and bottom of the intact band into clusters of four, using the same groupings as in the upper and lower hemstitched rows, group threads alternately at the top to bottom of the band. Secure the thread end in the side hem as before.

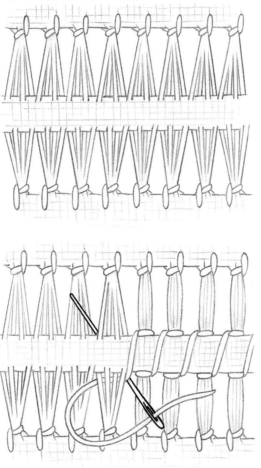

Tip

WITHDRAWING THREADS
If you find it difficult to pull the horizontal threads out of the fabric, try washing the material first to remove some of the manufacturer's dressing. Then snip the horizontal threads at regular intervals along the width of the fabric (allowing enough at each side to darn into the side hems) and use a pair of tweezers to pull out the cut threads.

Finishing the curtain

1 Stitching the heading Turn under 1.5cm (⅝in) along the remaining raw edge of the fabric, pin and tack. Knot the pull cords at one edge of the heading tape and leave them free at the other end. Tack and machine stitch the heading tape to the wrong side of the top edge, turning under the raw ends of the tape neatly and making sure you do not catch the loose cords in the stitching.

2 Finishing off Machine stitch the side hems. Remove all the tacking stitches and press the curtain on the wrong side using a hot iron with plenty of steam. Allow to dry, pull the loose ends of the cords up so the curtain fits the window, then knot the cords together to secure. Insert hooks and rings and hang the curtain on the rod.

Appliqué breakfast set

Chicken and egg motifs can only mean breakfast. Bold shapes
in bright fabrics appliquéd on to cheerful gingham create the
perfect setting to start the day.

A breakfast table set with a bright and sunny chicken tablecloth is a joy to get up to. Vivid checks make a perfect background for the jolly chickens; napkins and a matching tea-cosy echo the theme. For the tablecloth, napkins and tea-cosy, choose a gingham fabric with a large check, or a light-weight furnishing fabric with a printed or woven check. For the motifs, use remnants of printed and plain cotton dress fabrics in bright, primary colors. Check that they are pre-shrunk and colorfast before you start stitching.

▲ *Breakfast will definitely be a meal to linger over at a table laid with this jolly tablecloth, appliquéd with colorful and amusing chickens. You can make your own tablecloth from scratch or decorate a ready-made one.*

Making the tablecloth and napkins

The instructions below explain how to make a tablecloth and five napkins. The cloth is designed for a table about 130 x 100cm (79 x 39½in). To display the design properly, the tablecloth has a 40cm (15¾in) drop all around, so the actual size of the tablecloth is 210 x 180cm (83¼ x 71in). The napkins are 37cm (14½in) square. If your table is longer, or you wish to make some extra napkins, you will need to buy extra fabric. If you would rather embellish a ready-made tablecloth, omit steps 1-4.

Make sure the hemlines lie neatly on a line of checks. You can adjust the depth of the hem slightly if necessary. This also applies to the hemlines of the napkins and the base of the tea-cosy.

You will need

- 4.4m (5⅛yd) of checked cotton fabric, 137cm (55in) wide
- Matching thread
- Odds and ends of plain and printed cotton fabrics in primary colors
- Scraps of pre-washed calico
- White, red and turquoise soft cotton embroidery floss
- Tracing paper and pencil
- Bonding fabric, such as WonderUnder
- Chenille needle, size 22
- Sixteen flat white buttons, 1cm (⅜in) diameter

1 Cutting the gingham *For the tablecloth:* cut the fabric in half widthways. Put one piece aside for the central panel. Cut the other piece in half lengthways; take one part and cut this in half again lengthways for the side panels. *For the napkins:* cut the remaining fabric strip into 45cm (18in) squares.

2 Making the tablecloth Matching the pattern on the fabric and stitching along a line of checks, stitch one side panel to each long side of the central panel. Neaten the seam allowances, then press them open. Fold and press a 6cm (2¼in) double hem all around.

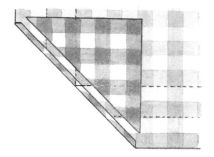

3 Mitering the corners Unfold the hem. Press up each corner so the diagonal crease runs through the intersection of the inner foldlines. Trim off each corner 6mm (¼in) from the diagonal crease.

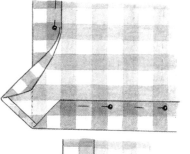

4 Finishing the miters Fold and press the hem again along each edge, making sure the diagonal folds of the miter meet neatly at the corner. Slipstitch the diagonal folds together. Then tack the hem to secure it in place temporarily.

5 Cutting out the motifs Trace the chicken, egg and leaf motifs on to tracing paper. Trace the leaf motif four times on to paper side of WonderUnder. Flip the tracing over and trace the leaf motif four more times. Work out how many chicken and egg motifs you want and trace each of these motifs the required number of times on to WonderUnder. Leaving a small margin around each shape, cut out the motifs.

6 Preparing fabric motifs Fuse the WonderUnder motifs to the wrong side of your chosen fabrics (see box below), using different fabrics for the chicken's legs, crest, body and beak; cut out. Peel off the paper backing.

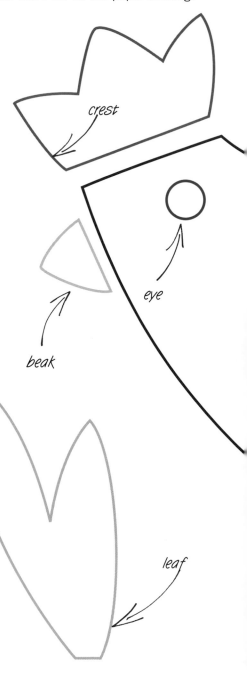

crest

eye

beak

leaf

Bonding motifs to fabric

Following manufacturer's instructions, place the WonderUnder rough (adhesive) side down on the wrong side of the motif fabric and press with a medium-hot, dry iron to bond the materials together. With the right side of the fabric upper-most, use small sharp scissors to cut out the motif. Peel off the backing paper and position the motif on the background fabric. Cover it with a damp cloth and press firmly with a medium-hot, dry iron. Leave the fabric to cool.

7 Placing the chicken motifs Pin the chickens, equally spaced, around the tablecloth, with the bottom of the feet resting on a line of checks about 11cm (4½ in) up from the edge. Make sure the top of the leg piece is tucked under the body, then vary the angle of the body for a more lively effect.

8 Finishing the appliqué Pin an egg between each chicken and in each corner. Add a leaf motif on each side of the corner eggs, making sure they face in opposite directions. Fuse all the motifs in place (see box on page 74).

9 Stitching the embroidery Using white soft cotton, work blanket stitch round the edge of each motif. Stitch the button eyes in place with turquoise soft cotton. With red soft cotton, work large running stitches all around the hem, just below the tacking line. Remove the tacking threads.

10 Making the napkins Fold and press a double 2cm (¾in) hem round the edges of each napkin square. Miter the corners and tack the hem as in steps **3-4**. Use red soft cotton and large running stitches to secure the hem in place, as in step **9**.

Full-size traccable patterns

body

egg

leg

▲ *Each motif of the chicken design is cut from a different fabric to give a cheerful effect, while blanket stitch, worked in soft cotton embroidery floss, adds a bold decorative finish to the design.*

Making the tea-cosy

The tea-cosy is made in two parts – a padded inner lining keeps the teapot warm, while the appliquéd cover slips on and off to allow for easy washing. Use calico for the lining, but make sure you wash it before you start.

You will need

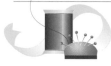

- 80 x 40cm (31½ x 15¾in) checked cotton fabric
- Odds and ends of plain and printed cotton fabrics
- Matching thread
- 50cm (⅝yd) lightweight pre-washed calico
- 70 x 40cm (27½ x 15¾in) of 400g (12oz) washable polyester batting
- Bonding fabric, such as WonderUnder
- One 1cm (⅜in) diameter flat white button
- White, red and turquoise soft embroidery floss
- Tracing paper, pencil and ruler
- Chenille needle, size 22

Traceable pattern

Top

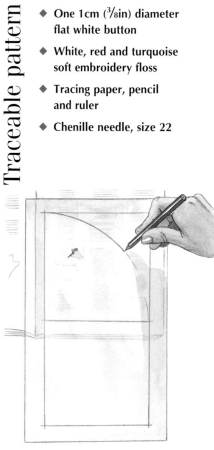

1 Making a pattern On tracing paper, draw a 31 x 17.5cm (12¼ x 6⅞in) rectangle. Place it over the traceable pattern, matching the top of the curve to the top of the rectangle. Trace the curve and cut out the paper pattern.

▲ *The jolly chicken makes another appearance, this time on the cover of a padded tea-cosy – you can relax and enjoy a slow and lingering breakfast, knowing your pot of tea will stay warm.*

2 Cutting out Fold the checked and calico fabrics on the straight grain; place the long straight edge of paper pattern on fold. *From checked fabric:* cut two pieces, adding 1cm (⅜in) to curved edge for seam allowances and 6cm (2¼in) to bottom for the hem. *From calico:* cut four pieces, adding 2cm (¾in) at the bottom for the hem. *From batting:* cut two pieces exactly to the size of the pattern.

3 Preparing the appliqué motifs Prepare one chicken and two leaf motifs, as in steps **5-6** on page 74, making sure the leaf motifs face in opposite directions.

4 Working the appliqué Position the chicken in the center of one checked tea-cosy piece on a line of checks as before, about 10cm (4in) up from the bottom edge. Fuse in place. Fuse a leaf on each side of the chicken, on same line of checks and 5cm (2in) in from the sides. Work the blanket stitch and attach the eye as in step **9** on page 75.

5 Finishing the cover Right sides together, and taking 1cm (⅜in) seam allowances, pin and machine stitch around the curved edges. Clip the seam allowances and press open. Turn through to the right side. Fold and tack a 3cm (1¼in) double hem, with the bottom of the hem on a line of checks. Secure with large running stitches in red soft cotton, as in step **9** on page 75.

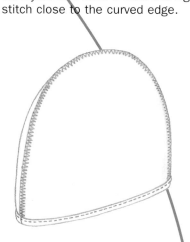

6 Making the lining With the curved edges matching, sandwich each batting piece between two calico pieces. Pin and tack firmly through all six layers and work a machine zigzag stitch close to the curved edge.

7 Finishing the lining On the bottom edge, turn a 1cm (⅜in) double hem and machine stitch close to the inner fold. Place inside the cover.

Cafetière cover

*Keep your coffee piping hot in true style with this sleek cosy,
specially designed to fit cafetières. Its crisp lines and amusing
details give it the dressy look of a smart waistcoat.*

Transport yourself to a café breakfast on the Champs Elysées with this chic cafetière cover, as elegantly dressed as a Paris waiter down to his red bowtie and buttons. Teamed with a matching tablecloth, the rich aroma of fresh coffee and wide café-au-lait cups, you can set a thoroughly continental breakfast table.

Choose your fabrics to match your table linen and china, but try to keep a continental flavor: dark blue, dark green or even black stripes or checks with white keep the right look. Dogtooth check would be fun, or you could go for a Paisley design on a small scale for a traditional luxury look. We used crisp white piqué for the contrast lining, but any plain cotton is suitable. Make sure the fabrics are washable; it's a good idea to make two so you can rotate them for washing.

▼ *Snappy red and white check is a perfect choice for this distinctly Gallic style breakfast table. The cafetière cover is finished with a flourish – gleaming white piqué lapels, smart red buttons and a dickie bow.*

Making the cafetière cover

The cover is made from two batted sections joined together at the front and held at the back with a tab fixed with Velcro. These instructions make a cover to fit a cafetière 10cm (4in) in diameter and about 20cm (8in) high – check that your cafetière is a similar size or adapt the pattern to fit. When pressing the cover, use a low heat and gentle pressure to avoid flattening the batting too much.

You will need

- ◆ 25cm (10in) main fabric
- ◆ 25cm (10in) contrast fabric
- ◆ 25cm (10in) mediumweight batting
- ◆ Matching threads
- ◆ 20cm (8in) of 2.5cm (1in) wide ribbon
- ◆ Two small buttons
- ◆ One Velcro spot
- ◆ Tracing paper

▲ *The cover wraps snugly around a standard cafetière, fastening with a Velcro tab at the back. Measure your cafetière before starting to make sure that the cover will fit. You can adapt the template by altering the length from the stitching line to the tabbed edge.*

1 Cutting out Trace the template from page 79, marking in the stitching line and foldlines, and cut out. Adding 1cm (⅜in) seam allowance all around, cut two pieces in batting. On the right side of the main fabric pieces, transfer the markings with the dressmaker's pencil.

2 Making the tab Cut a piece of main fabric 4.5cm (1¾in) square and fold in half right sides together. Stitch one long and one short side, taking a 1cm (⅜in) seam. Trim the seam allowances and turn to the right side. On the main fabric piece, pin the tab in the marked position, matching raw edges.

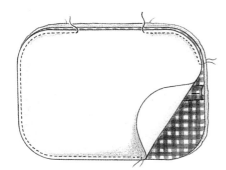

3 Joining the layers Pin the main fabric piece right sides together with its lining, sandwiching the tab, with the batting underneath. Taking a 1cm (⅜in) seam, pin and stitch all around, leaving a 7.5cm (3in) gap to turn. Repeat with the other pieces, omitting the tab.

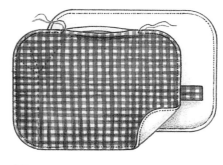

4 Topstitching the edges On each section, snip out small notches on the seam allowances at the curves to reduce bulk. Turn the two sections right side out, and press, turning the edges in carefully at the gaps. Using a contrast thread, topstitch all around 3mm (⅛in) from the edge.

5 Stitching the front seam Place the two sections lining sides together and pin along the stitching line. Stitch, reversing at top and bottom.

Full-size traceable template

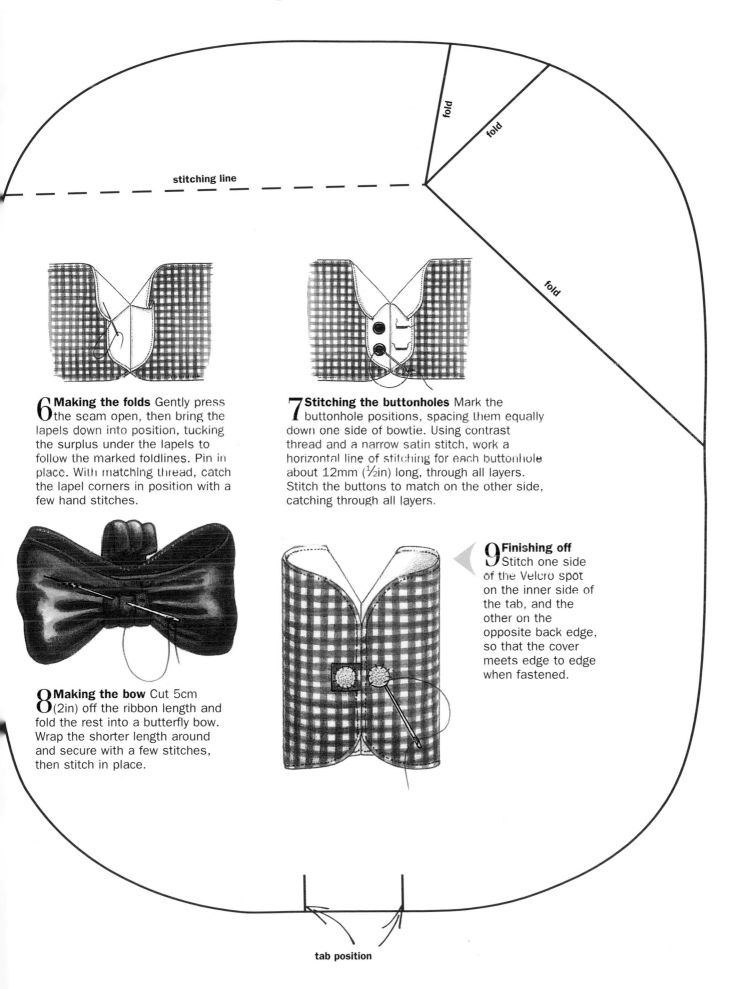

fold

fold

fold

stitching line

6 Making the folds Gently press the seam open, then bring the lapels down into position, tucking the surplus under the lapels to follow the marked foldlines. Pin in place. With matching thread, catch the lapel corners in position with a few hand stitches.

7 Stitching the buttonholes Mark the buttonhole positions, spacing them equally down one side of bowtie. Using contrast thread and a narrow satin stitch, work a horizontal line of stitching for each buttonhole about 12mm ($\frac{1}{2}$in) long, through all layers. Stitch the buttons to match on the other side, catching through all layers.

8 Making the bow Cut 5cm (2in) off the ribbon length and fold the rest into a butterfly bow. Wrap the shorter length around and secure with a few stitches, then stitch in place.

9 Finishing off Stitch one side of the Velcro spot on the inner side of the tab, and the other on the opposite back edge, so that the cover meets edge to edge when fastened.

tab position

Making a coiled mat

These smart and practical mats make striking table accessories and can be made for next to nothing, using up odd strips of fabric and batting. As they are all sewn by hand, it's the sort of thing you can do while relaxing with the TV or music. You can make them as big or as small as you like, depending on the length of the coil, and vary the thickness too by making a thicker roll for extra protection.

As a guide, the larger mat measures 15cm (6in) diameter and is made from a 140cm (55in) coil. The smaller one measures 13.5cm (5¼in) and uses a 132cm (52in) length. The fabric strips are cut on the bias, and these instructions are for a mat about 1.5cm (⅝in) deep, 15cm (6in) across. Mediumweight batting is used here; if you have lightweight batting scraps, cut the strips twice as wide.

To make the smaller mat, stitch together contrasting bias strips 5cm (2in) wide. Cut into strips in the opposite direction to make the bias strips for the coiled length.

▲ *Strips of bias cut fabric wrapped around batting rolls make useful and decorative table mats. Choose fabrics that will complement your table linen.*

You will need

- ◆ Offcuts of fabric
- ◆ Offcuts of mediumweight batting
- ◆ Matching thread
- ◆ Needle and pins

1 Cutting the strips Cut a bias strip of fabric 7cm (2¾in) wide, measuring 140cm (55in) long. Cut a 10cm (4in) wide strip of batting the same length, or two or three pieces to make up the length.

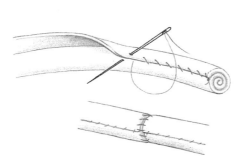

2 Making the batting roll Thread the needle with double thread. Starting at one end, roll the batting into a sausage and secure with large oversewing stitches. Work to the end, keeping the roll smooth and even. Join any pieces if necessary by butting up together and oversewing after rolling.

3 Covering the roll On one edge of the bias strip, press under a 1cm (⅜in) hem. Wrap the strip around the roll, bringing the pressed hem over the raw edge, with the batting end 1cm (⅜in) in from the end of the fabric strip. Pin all along the roll, and slipstitch in place.

▶ *Joining short pieces to make the long strip gives an interesting staggered effect – and uses your smallest scraps.*

4 Starting the coil Thread the needle with matching double thread. Turn the raw fabric edges in at the end and slipstitch; with the seam on the inside, curl the coil tightly round on itself, and secure with a stitch or two.

5 Completing the mat Continue coiling, working ladder stitch between the previous coil and the next one as you go, and keeping the seam hidden between the coils. Flatten the mat on the table from time to time to keep the shape even. At the end, turn the raw edges in and slipstitch closed.

Fabric clothespins bag

*Keep your clothespins handy in this
attractive bag while you're hanging out
the washing on the line.*

Roomy enough to store plenty of clothespins and even a clothesline if necessary, this bag is a smart and practical addition to your home laundry equipment. You can make it from a remnant of fabric and a standard wooden coathanger. The bag is simple to put together, using equipment you already have.

Mediumweight printed or plain fabrics with a firm, close weave are ideal for the bag, such as cotton, cotton/polyester, linen, linen/polyester and linen/cotton, with plain, twill or piqué weaves. Because the bag usually stays outside while in use, the fabric you choose needs to be colorfast. Wash and press a small piece of fabric beforehand if you are not sure.

Check that the hook on the coat-hanger twists around easily, so that the bag will be able to swivel around in the wind; if you use a hook that doesn't rotate, the bag will blow off the line.

▼ *This handy clothespin bag is made from a mediumweight cotton in a colorfast daisy-print; the opening is faced and topstitched for extra strength.*

Making the clothespin bag

The bag is made from one piece of fabric, with the fold at the bottom of the bag and seams at the top and sides. The fabric at the top is slightly curved to fit the shape of the coathanger, and a small gap is left in the seaming at the top to allow the coathanger hook to be slotted through. The 'letterbox' opening is faced with matching fabric, and then topstitched for added strength. The raw edges of the facing are neatened with a narrow hem, but you could zigzag or overlock them if you prefer. The completed bag measures 42cm (16½in) wide and 33cm (13in) long; use 1cm (⅜in) seam allowances throughout.

You will need

- ◆ 70cm (¾yd) of 90cm (33in) wide firmly woven, mediumweight cotton fabric or an 80 x 44cm (31 x 18in) remnant
- ◆ Standard wooden coathanger
- ◆ Matching sewing threads
- ◆ Scissors
- ◆ Pencil

1 Cutting out the fabric Press the fabric and straighten the edges if necessary. *For the bag:* cut out a rectangle measuring 69 x 44cm (27 x 17½in) with the grainline parallel to the longest side of the rectangle. *For the opening facing:* cut a second rectangle measuring 8 x 33cm (3½ x 13in).

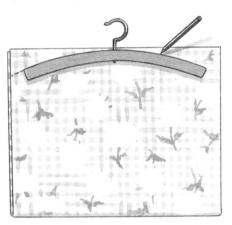

2 Shaping the bag Fold the main fabric in half widthways, right sides together. Place the coathanger centrally along the raw edges and, holding it firmly, draw around the top edge of the hanger with a pencil. Pin the two fabrics together and cut around the curved edge.

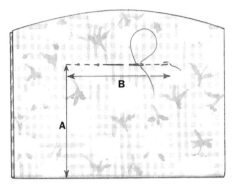

3 Marking the letterbox opening Measure 23cm (9in) up from the bottom fold (**A**) and using pins, mark a horizontal line 23cm (9in) long (**B**). Make sure the ends of the line are the same distance from the sides of the bag and pin through the top layer of fabric only. Tack along the line through a single thickness of fabric only. Remove all pins.

4 Stitching the facing On the facing, neaten the edges by machine stitching a single 6mm (¼in) turning all around: the two short edges first, followed by the long edges. With right sides together, pin and tack the facing centrally over the tacked line. Working on the wrong side of the main bag piece, machine stitch a rectangle 2 x 23cm (¾ x 9in) around the line of marker tacking stitches.

5 Turning the facing through Use scissors to cut along the center of the rectangle and diagonally into the corners, close to the stitches. Turn the facing through the opening, pulling the short ends to form the rectangular letterbox opening. Press the seam flat and topstitch 3mm (⅛in) in from the seam, and then again 3mm (⅛in) inside that to double topstitch the opening and add strength.

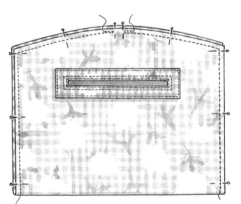

6 Seaming the bag With right sides together, pin around all three sides, leaving a small central gap about 1cm (⅜in) long. Stitch together, using reverse stitch for 1.5cm (⅝in) at beginning and end. Snip across the corners. Finger-press the seam, turn through and press on the right side.

Fabric-covered bulletin boards

A bulletin board can serve as the memory-jogging center of your household – a place to file vital telephone numbers, forthcoming invitations, outstanding bills and important dates.

◄ *Covered in cheerful gingham with a criss-cross of white cotton tapes, this snazzy bulletin board is bound to attract your attention to its messages and reminders.*

A regularly consulted bulletin board can play an important part in keeping your home running smoothly. Covering it in fabric helps to make it look less businesslike and blend in with its surroundings – or stand out and catch everyone's eye. Adding a diagonal trellis of ribbons or tapes, held in place with decorative upholstery nails, avoids the use of pins that might damage the fabric – you simply slip items behind the criss-crossed ribbons.

You can make the bulletin board square or rectangular, to any size you like, depending on the room you have to hang it. Space aside, the best location for a bulletin board is determined by the nature and quantity of the information you are going to display. Emergency numbers, to get hold of the plumber quickly for example, are best kept near to the telephone; as the family coordination center, the board is probably best hung in the kitchen. Remember to go over the board frequently, so that it doesn't get congested with out-of-date leaflets and notes.

▲ *Fix small, decorative screwhooks, sold for holding tiebacks, to a smaller version of the bulletin board for a handy keyholder. You can arrange the hooks in neat rows or randomly. To make a keyholder, use the instructions on the following page, reducing the size of the board accordingly.*

Covering a bulletin board

To make this bulletin board economically, you can use up fabric remnants from a previous soft furnishings project. For a softer, more padded look, cover the board with an interlining, such as lightweight bump or domette, before adding the fabric. Staple it over the board in the same way as the main fabric.

Inexpensive 12mm (½in) thick softboard or insulation board is an ideal base, being soft enough to push pins in easily, yet robust enough to hold them firmly and light enough to hang from a picture hook. You can buy a piece cut to size at a lumber or DIY store, or cut your own with a sharp craft knife.

A staple gun is the speediest way of anchoring the fabric to the back of the board. Alternatively, you can use panel pins to hold the fabric securely.

You will need

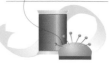

- ◆ **460mm (18in) square of softboard or insulation board, 12mm (½in) thick**
- ◆ **58cm (23in) square piece of cotton fabric**
- ◆ **Staple gun or panel pins and a hammer**
- ◆ **5m (5½yd) of ribbon, tape or braid, 12mm (½in) wide**
- ◆ **13 decorative upholstery nails**
- ◆ **2 picture rings, cord and hook**

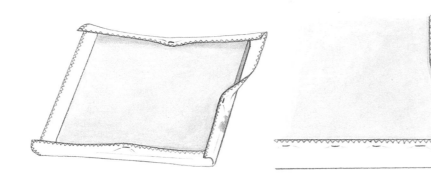

1 Attaching the fabric Neaten the edge of the fabric with zigzag stitch and lay it, right side down, on a flat surface. Place the board centrally on top and wrap one edge of fabric to the wrong side. Secure it with a staple or hammer a panel pin in the center. Pulling the fabric taut, secure the center of the opposite side in the same way. Repeat for remaining two sides.

2 Covering the board Working outwards from the center, on each side in turn, add further staples or panel pins at 5cm (2in) intervals, stopping 10cm (4in) from each corner. Take care to keep the fabric even and taut on the right side of the board.

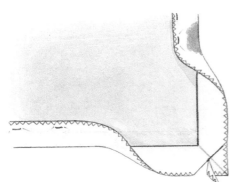

3 Trimming the corners On the wrong side of the fabric, draw a line from one corner of the board to the matching corner of the fabric. Measure and mark the depth of the board plus 6mm (¼in) along the line from the corner of the board. Cut straight across the corner of the fabric at this point. Repeat for the remaining corners.

4 Mitering the corners Wrap one cut edge of the fabric over a corner and secure temporarily with a dressmaker's pin. Fold in each side of the fabric to meet neatly along the corner-to-corner diagonal, stapling up to the corner and down sides of the folds. Remove pin. Repeat to miter the remaining corners.

5 Attaching the first ribbon Lay the first ribbon diagonally across the right side of the board from corner to corner. Leaving an extra 5cm (2in) at each end, cut the ribbon to fit. Wrap one raw end round to the wrong side of the board, turn under 1cm (⅜in) and staple in place. Keeping the ribbon taut, secure the other end in the same way. Repeat for the opposite diagonal.

▼ *A close trellis of picot-edged grosgrain ribbon, held by antiqued brass upholstery nails, adds an extra decorative quality to these fabric-covered bulletin boards.*

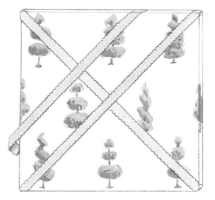

6 Fixing the other ribbons Attach further ribbons parallel to the second ribbon in the same way, about 15cm (6in) apart. When all ribbons in one direction are fixed, repeat in the opposite direction. Add an upholstery nail wherever the ribbons cross.

7 Hanging the board Attach hanging rings about a quarter of the way down each side of the board. Tie cord between the rings and hang the board from a picture hook.

Austrian blinds

With their soft, undulating folds, Austrian blinds are a classic favorite for smaller windows. Make a simple version to show off a strong pattern, or add a flirty frill for a feminine look.

Austrian blinds are gathered at the top with heading tape, like any ordinary curtain, but there the resemblance ends. The lower edge is permanently drawn up in a series of deep swags; when the blind is raised, cords hidden at the back draw the remaining fabric into sweeping folds.

When these blinds first appeared in the 18th century, they were made in velvet and silk and lavishly trimmed with fringes and tassels. These days, chintzes and dainty frills are more popular. This style is ideal for bathroom windows. For a contemporary twist, make a plain and simple blind in a feature fabric – a strong black and white design, perhaps, or a splashy, modern abstract print.

▼ *The soft, puffy folds of Austrian blinds complement a pretty blue and white fabric, ideal for the bathroom. Add a frill for extra effect.*

Making an Austrian blind

These instructions explain how to make an unlined blind. If you want to line the blind for a fuller look, add the lining before stitching on the tapes.

Hang your blind from an Austrian blind track: this has runners for hooks like a curtain track, plus special rings to carry the cords. You can fix the track directly to the wall, or fit a batten first.

For the vertical gathers, use Austrian blind tape, which has loops or rings for threading the cords through. For the gathered heading, use any standard pencil pleat curtain heading tape.

To neaten the cord ends, thread them through a hollow wooden knob, called an acorn, and secure them to a cleat fixed to the side of the window.

Calculating quantities

Fabric For the best effect, make the blind really full. Allow 2½ times the width of the track, plus 6cm (2¼in) for each side hem – you may need as much as two or three widths of fabric. For the cut length, allow the height of the window plus 45cm (18in); this will give you enough length for the blind to remain swagged at the base edge when it is lowered, and includes allowances for turnings as well.

Tape and cord First decide how many swags you'd like along the bottom. The cords which create the swags are usually set about 60-70cm (24-28in) apart across the ungathered fabric; this will give 24-30cm (9-12in) wide swags when the heading tape is gathered up. Choose a swag size which divides evenly into the width of your track.

You will need a length of Austrian blind tape (blue in diagram) to run down between each swag and down each side edge; add 2.5cm (1in) to each tape for turnings.

For each cord (red in diagram),

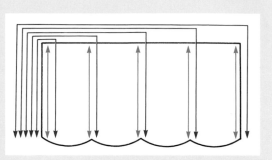

double the length of the corresponding tape and add the distance from the top of the tape to the corner of the blind on the cleat side.

You will need

- ◆ Furnishing fabric
- ◆ Pencil pleat heading tape
- ◆ Austrian blind tape
- ◆ Blind cord
- ◆ Matching thread
- ◆ Austrian blind track
- ◆ Cleat and acorn
- ◆ Cord joiner (optional)
- ◆ Dressmaker's pencil

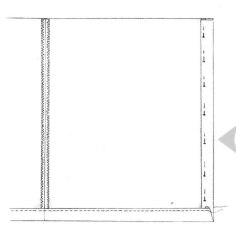

1 Measuring up Fit the track in position. Measure the track width (**A**) and the length from the top of the track to the sill (**B**). Fit the cleat on the wall at a comfortable height.

2 Cutting out Referring to *Calculating quantities* above, cut enough widths of fabric to make a piece the required size of the blind.

3 Seaming up Right sides together, join all the fabric widths; neaten seams and press open. On each side edge, press under 1cm (⅜in) then 5cm (2in); pin, but do not stitch. Repeat to hem the lower edge, folding the corners in neat miters. Stitch this hem only.

4 Cutting the tapes Lay the blind out flat, with the fabric wrong side up. Measure from the top of the hem to the top edge, and add 1cm (⅜in). Cut the required number of pieces of Austrian blind tape to this length, measuring each time from 1cm (⅜in) below a loop or ring.

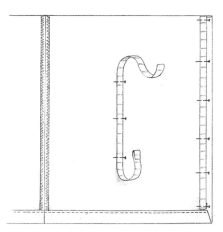

5 Placing the tapes Place a length of Austrian blind tape on one side edge; position the tape so that its outer edge overlaps the inner fold of the side hem; at the bottom of the tape, turn under 1cm (⅜in) and position the first loop or ring just above the hem; pin to hold. Repeat to pin another length of tape at the other side edge. Space the other tapes evenly across the blind, making sure that all the loops or rings line up horizontally; pin.

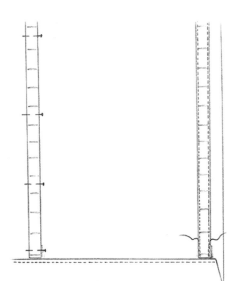

6 Stitching the tapes Stitch down each edge of the side tapes, securing the side hems at the same time, and backstitching at the bottom for strength. Stitch all the other tapes in the same way.

7 Adding the heading tape Lay out the blind, right side up. Measuring up from the bottom edge, mark the window length **B** plus 30cm (12in), and press under. Referring to the box on page 88 and enclosing the top of the Austrian blind tapes, apply the heading tape, and gather it up to fit the track.

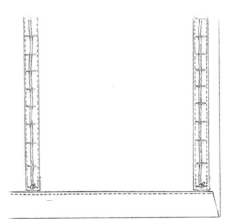

8 Threading the cords For each vertical tape, cut a length of cord long enough to run up the tape, across the top of the blind and down the side. On each tape, knot the cord to the bottom loop or ring and thread it up through the loops to the top.

9 Mounting the blind Adjust the position of the eyelets on the track to match the tapes on the blind. Insert curtain hooks and hang the blind. Starting on the side furthest from the cleat, thread each cord through the corresponding eyelet, then through all the other eyelets.

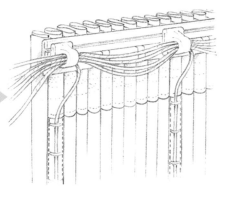

▲ *With their voluptuous folds, Austrian blinds create a soft, pretty outline, and are often a more practical option for bathrooms than curtains.*

10 Finishing off Raise blind fully and even up the cord tensions, then lower it to the sill and adjust again. Knot the cords at the end of the track. Plait them together to make a single cord, or use a cord joiner. Trim the ends and fit an acorn.

Making a frilled Austrian blind

Adding a frill to your blind will give it an even softer outline, either in the same or a contrasting color. In this version, the 7.5cm (3in) frill is made from a layer of fabric with contrast binding on both edges. You can use ready-made bias binding – just pick a color from your fabric. You will need all the materials listed on the previous page, plus fabric for the frill and contrast bias binding. To work out the quantity of binding, add the base of the blind to twice the length and multiply by five.

1 Cutting out Following steps **1-2** on the page 86, measure up and cut out the blind, but add 4cm (1½in) to **A** and 40cm (15¾in) to **B**.

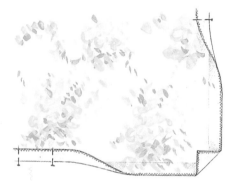

2 Seaming up Right sides together, join all the fabric widths, neaten the seams and press them open. Neaten the sides and base edge. Then press 2cm (¾in) towards the front on these edges, folding the corners into neat miters; pin.

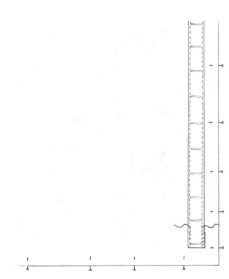

3 Adding the tapes As in steps **4-6** on pages 86-87, apply the Austrian blind tapes on the wrong side of the blind, but set the bottom loops 2.5cm (1in) above the base edge of the blind, and the side tapes 2.5cm (1in) in from the side edges.

Adding heading tape

Positioning the tape Cut a length of heading tape as described in step **7** on page 87. On the wrong side, center and pin the heading tape along the top of the blind, 1cm (⅜in) down from the top. Pin along the lower edge of the tape too, trimming the edge of the fabric if necessary so that it is covered by the tape.

Neatening the tape At one end, pull out the tape cords from the wrong side of the tape and knot them together securely. Turn under 2.5cm (1in) at the end of the tape, covering the knotted cords. At the other end, pull out the cords on the right side of the tape and leave them free. Turn under 2.5cm (1in) of tape.

Stitching the tape To prevent puckering, stitch along the top and bottom edges of the heading tape in the same direction. Then, leaving the two cords free at one end, stitch across the ends of the tape.

Gathering the blind Pull up the loose cord ends evenly until the blind is gathered to the right width. Make a knot in the cords near the heading tape to hold the gathers. Wind the surplus cords round a cord tidy or into a neat bundle. Slip the cord tidy into the heading tape or catch the wound cord with two stitches to the top of the blind.

4 Adding the heading tape Apply the heading tape as in step **7** on page 87, but start and end 1cm (⅜in) in from the pressed side edges.

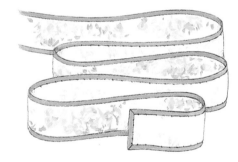

5 Making the frill Cut enough 7.5cm (3in) wide pieces of the frill fabric to go 2½ times round the sides and base of the blind when joined up. Right sides together, join all the pieces; neaten the seams and press them open. Apply bias binding to all four sides of the frill, mitering the corners neatly.

6 Gathering the frill Divide the frill into four equal lengths and mark. Stitching 2cm (¾in) in from one edge and stopping and starting at each pin, run a gathering thread the length of the frill. Measure round the sides and bottom edge of the blind; divide into four and mark.

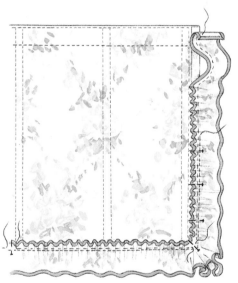

7 Applying the frill Lay out the blind, right side up. Pin the frill, right side up, round the side and base edges, aligning the frill ends with the top of the blind and centering the gathering line over the pressed hem. Pull up the gathers to fit; stitch.

8 Finishing off Thread the cords, mount the blind and adjust it, as in steps **8-10** on page 87.

Sheer pocket curtain

Stitch a sheer fabric curtain, with a scattering of translucent ribbon pockets and a buttoned tab heading. Fill the pockets with small sprays of fragrant lavender.

This pretty curtain makes a delightful window screen for the bathroom. The sheer fabric provides a gentle, diffused light, and the stitched pockets feature sprigs of fragrant lavender, which scent the room. The curtain consists of a hemmed rectangle of sheer fabric, suspended from the rod or pole with sheer ribbon tabs. The tabs are cut to length, then secured in place with buttons stitched through all the fabric layers. The pockets are cut from a strip of wider sheer ribbon, then zigzag-stitched in place along the side and base edges.

For the main curtain, choose a closely woven sheer fabric that will support the pockets without pulling out of shape. You'll find a wide range of sheer ribbons in fabric and craft stores. Choose a ribbon color to match your main fabric, or opt for a contrast. To avoid marking the fabrics, use fine dressmaker's pins.

The pockets on the curtain featured here are filled with small sprays of lavender, but you can substitute any items of your own choice provided they are lightweight. Little seashells, pressed flowers, bay leaves and other herbs are good alternatives. You could also change the content according to the seasons.

▲ *A sheer silk café curtain with dainty ribbon pockets creates a pretty screen at the window, where it filters the light. Sprays of lavender in the pockets add charming detailing and scent the air with their heady fragrance.*

Making a sheer pocket curtain

You will need

- Sheer fabric
- Sheer ribbon, 2.5cm (1in) and 10cm (4in) wide
- Matching sewing thread
- Tape measure
- Fine dressmaker's pins
- Lightweight buttons
- Handsewing needle
- Pinking shears
- Sprays of lavender

Measuring and cutting out

Curtain length Measure from a point just below the pole or rod (where the top of the curtain will lie), to the desired curtain length. Add 10cm (4in) for the top hem, and at least 10cm (4in) for the base hem.

Curtain width Measure the length of the pole or rod. Multiply by 1½ if you want some fullness. Add 6cm (2¼in) for side hems.

Ribbon tabs Decide on the desired length of the tabs: these should be long enough to go round the curtain pole or rod, and overlap the top of the curtain by 4cm (1½in) at each end, plus leave a hanging space between the pole and curtain top. From 2.5cm (1in) wide ribbon, cut the required number of tabs to this length.

Ribbon pockets From 10cm (4in) wide ribbon, cut the desired number of 17cm (6¾in) lengths – one length for each pocket.

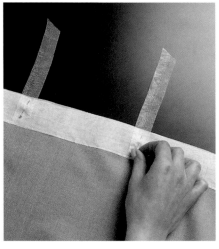

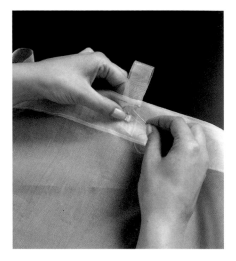

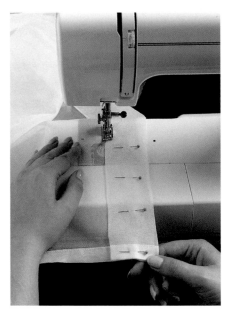

1 Hemming the curtain Turn under a double 1.5cm (⅝in) hem down each side edge. Pin then stitch. Turn under and stitch a double 5cm (2in) hem at the top edge of the curtain.

2 Positioning the tabs Lay the curtain out flat, wrong side up. Position one tab ribbon at each end of the top edge, lined up with the side edges, short ends lying just above the base of the hem. Space the remainder evenly in-between. Pin in place.

3 Stitching the tabs Turn the curtain over to lie right side up. Bring the tabs over to the front and pin in place to form loops. Check the loop size, then secure by stitching a button through all the fabric layers, with the buttons positioned approximately halfway down the heading hem.

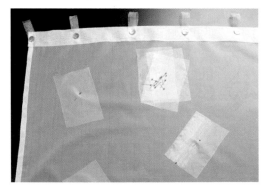

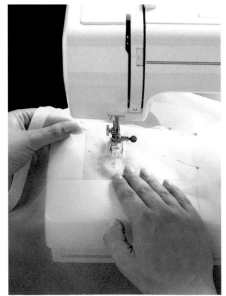

4 Positioning the pockets Hang the curtain in place on the pole. Pin the bottom hem, take down and stitch by hand or machine. Lay the curtain out flat, right side up, and arrange the lengths of wide ribbon on it. Pin them in place.

5 Stitching the pockets Lift off one of the pockets. Use pinking shears to trim across both short ends for a decorative finish. Fold under approximately 2cm (¾in) at each end of the ribbon, one end to go on the inside and the other outside. Pin then tack the pocket in place on the curtain, so that the top edge is folded out and the base edge folded in. Set your sewing machine to a medium-width zigzag stitch, and stitch the pocket in place down the sides and across the base edge. Repeat for each pocket. Insert a small spray of lavender into each pocket.

Shower curtains

Brighten up your bathroom with a distinctive shower curtain. Make the curtain from showerproof fabric, or from a colorful furnishing fabric teamed with a separate showerproof curtain liner.

Making your own shower curtain allows you more flexibility in both choosing a fabric and deciding on a curtain style. You can make the curtain either from showerproof fabric, which is available in a range of plain colors and patterns, or use a washable furnishing fabric teamed with a showerproof curtain liner. Use an inexpensive, ready-made shower curtain for the liner or make your own from showerproof fabric.

You can make a standard shower curtain with a punched eyelet heading, or give it an individual stamp – by adding a contrasting valance, for example, or by using buttonholes rather than eyelets for the heading. Both these options are shown overleaf. If you want to use eyelets, you can buy an eyelet kit with full instructions from fabric or craft stores. A range of eyelet sizes and metal colors is available.

Shower curtains are usually hung in place using special plastic, vinyl or metal shower curtain rings, slotted through the holes across the top of the curtain. You can buy the rings from bathroom fixtures and fittings departments in large stores.

▶ *A shower curtain made from bright waterproof fabric is an excellent way to add an invigorating touch to a bathroom or shower-room scheme.*

◀ *You can hang your shower curtain the traditional way – by slotting shower-curtain rings through the eyelet or buttonhole heading; or lace it in place using nylon cord for an original alternative.*

Shower curtain with separate valance

You will need

- ◆ Showerproof or furnishing fabric
- ◆ Contrasting showerproof or furnishing fabric for the valance (optional)

- ◆ Tape measure
- ◆ Pins
- ◆ Matching sewing thread
- ◆ Eyelet kit (optional)

Measuring and cutting out

Cut curtain length Measure from the underside of the shower rail to the desired curtain length. Add 25cm (10in).
Cut curtain width Allow 1-1½ times the length of the shower rail plus 10cm (4in) for side hems, and 1.6cm (⅝in) seam allowances if joining fabric widths.
Cut valance length Add 15cm (6in) to the desired valance length.
Cut valance width is the same as the cut curtain width.

1 Joining fabric widths Use French seams. Place the fabric wrong sides together. Pin then stitch a 6mm (¼in) seam. Press the seam allowance to one side.

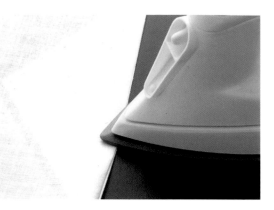

2 Pressing the seamline Fold the fabric right sides together along the seamline, enclosing the seam allowance. Press.

3 Stitching along the seam Stitch 1cm (⅜in) from the folded edge, enclosing the first seam. Press the seam to one side.

4 Hemming the curtain Press under a double 7.5cm (3in) hem on the bottom edge of the curtain, and machine stitch close to the inner fold. Press under a double 2.5cm (1in) hem on each side edge of the curtain, and machine stitch.

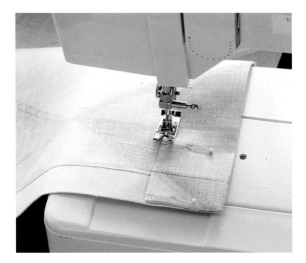

5 Hemming the top Press under a double 5cm (2in) hem on the upper edge of the curtain, and machine stitch close to the inner fold.

6 Positioning the eyelets Use pins to mark the positions of the eyelets or buttonholes on the top edge of the curtain. If using a ready-made shower-curtain liner, match the pin marks to the position of the holes in the liner. Alternatively, place the pins 2cm (¾in) from the top edge of the curtain and about 16cm (6¼in) apart, with the first and last pin marks 4cm (1½in) from each side edge.

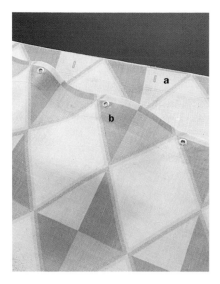

7 Adding the eyelets Either machine stitch a 1.3cm (½in) vertical buttonhole (a) at each pin mark, with the upper end of the buttonhole at the mark (see your sewing machine manual for how to machine stitching buttonholes); or attach an eyelet (b) at each mark, following the eyelet kit manufacturer's instructions.

8 Making the valance Make the valance in the same way as the shower curtain, following steps **1-7**, but stitch a 2.5cm (1in) double hem on the bottom edge of the valance. Match up the holes in the curtain and valance, and insert the shower curtain rings through both layers as shown.

Shower curtain with attached valance

You will need

- ◆ **Showerproof or furnishing fabric**
- ◆ **Contrasting showerproof or furnishing fabric for the valance (optional)**
- ◆ **Tape measure and pins**
- ◆ **Matching sewing thread**
- ◆ **Eyelet kit (optional)**

Measuring and cutting out

Cut curtain length Measure from the underside of the shower rail to the desired curtain length. Add 15cm (6in) to this measurement.

Cut curtain width Allow 1-1½ times the length of the shower rail, plus 10cm (4in) for side hems, and 1.6cm (⅝ in) seam allowances if joining fabric widths.

Cut valance length Add 11.5cm (4½in) to the desired valance length.

Cut valance width is the same as the cut curtain width.

1 Making the valance Follow steps **1-4**, for both the shower curtain and the valance, but stitch a double 2.5cm (1in) hem on the bottom edge of the valance. On the upper edge of the valance, press under 1.3cm (½in) then 5cm (2in).

2 Pinning valance to curtain Place the curtain right side down on wrong side of the valance, with the upper edge level with the folded edge of the valance. Fold the upper edge of the valance over the curtain; pin in place through all layers.

3 Stitching valance to curtain Stitch close to the bottom folded edge of the valance, securing the curtain between the layers of the valance.

4 Adding the eyelets Add eyelets or stitch buttonholes through the upper edge of the shower curtain and valance, as in steps **6-7**.

Department stores and fabric stores stock a range of showerproof fabrics. Choose one to coordinate with your bathroom or shower room. Here, a white curtain printed with old-fashioned taps is a stylish and individual choice, and ties in with the white and blue color scheme.

Showerproof fabric with a snappy geometric design makes a stylish shower curtain for this streamlined, functional bathroom.

A contrast valance adds an attractive detail at the top of a shower curtain. You can make a separate valance, or stitch it in place, as here. As a guide, make the valance approximately one-sixth the overall length of the shower curtain.

Vanity skirts

Transform a washbasin with a gathered skirt. Quick to make and fixed in place with a touch-and-close fastener, it makes a pretty addition to a bathroom.

Attach a gathered fabric vanity skirt round a washbasin to create an attractive feature and to hide unsightly under-sink plumbing in the bathroom. You can also transform a basic side table by adding a vanity skirt, which will provide a useful hidden storage area in the bathroom. Choose a fabric that coordinates with the other soft furnishings in the room – matching it to the curtains or window blind, for example.

A vanity skirt is very easy to make. It consists of a piece of hemmed fabric that is gathered on to a band of fabric along its upper edge, then attached with touch-and-close fastening. Depending on the style of the basin, you can attach the skirt to the outside or inside edge as shown overleaf. The positioning of table legs often means a table skirt has to be attached to the outside edge.

Usually the skirt runs around the sides and front of the sink or table. However, when using an inside mount you may prefer to extend the skirt a short way along the back for a neater finish. If a table stands away from the wall, or is round or oval in shape, you may want to continue the skirt all the way around the back.

▼ *Attaching a vanity skirt around a washbasin is a practical way to hide unsightly pipes. It also creates a hidden storage area for cleaning materials and bathroom paraphernalia.*

Making a vanity skirt

You will need

- Pencil or felt-tipped pen
- Tape measure
- Stick-and-stitch, touch-and-close fastening
- Furnishing fabric
- Matching sewing thread
- Fine cord, such as pearl cotton thread

Measuring and cutting out

Stick the touch-and-close fastening in place following step **1**, before measuring and cutting out the fabric.

Cut skirt length Measure from the lower edge of the touch-and-close fastening to 1.3cm (½in) above the floor. Add 6.5cm (2½in) to this measurement for hem and seam allowances.

Cut skirt width Measure round the washbasin or table along the fastening to find the finished skirt width. Multiply this measurement by 2½.

Skirt band Cut a strip of fabric measuring 7.5cm (3in) wide by the finished skirt width plus 2.5cm (1in).

Positioning the vanity skirt

Outside edge You can attach the skirt to the outside edge of most washbasins and dressing tables.

Inside edge On some washbasins you can attach the skirt to the inside edge. However, the legs of a table may make this impossible.

1 Positioning the fastening tape Mark a line all around the inside or outside edge of the sink or table, making sure it is parallel with the floor. Fix the sticky side of the fastening tape along the line.

2 Cutting and hemming the fabric Cut and join fabric widths taking 1.3cm (½in) seams, to make up the skirt length and width. Press under a double 2.5cm (1in) hem on the lower edge and machine stitch. Press under a 1.3cm (½in) double hem on each side and machine stitch.

3 Positioning the cord Position the fine cord just inside the 1.3cm (½in) seamline along the upper raw edge of the skirt. Zigzag stitch over the cord.

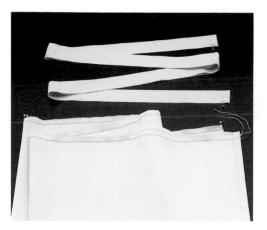

4 Pinning on the skirt band Divide the upper edge of the skirt into four and mark with pins. Press the skirt band in half lengthways with right sides together and long edges matching. Measure 1.3cm (½in) from each short end of the band and mark with pins. Divide the band between the pins into four and mark again.

5 Tacking on the band Unfold the band and position it along the upper edge of the skirt with right sides together. Match the end pins on the band with the side edges of the skirt then match the remaining pins. Pull up the gathering cord to fit. Pin and tack.

6 Joining the band to the skirt Stitch the skirt and band together, taking a 1.3cm (½in) seam. Press the seam allowances towards the band.

7 Attaching the tape Place the remaining side of the touch-and-close tape on the right side of the band, 3mm (⅛in) from the pressed center line of the band. If attaching the skirt to the outside edge, place the fastening on the lower half of the band, next to the skirt (a). If attaching to the inside edge, place it on the upper half (b). Pin then stitch along both long edges of the fastening through one layer of fabric only, stitching both rows in the same direction.

8 Finishing the band hems Press under 1cm (⅜in) on the unstitched long edge. Right sides together, fold along center line. Stitch 1.3cm (½in) seams across both short ends; trim.

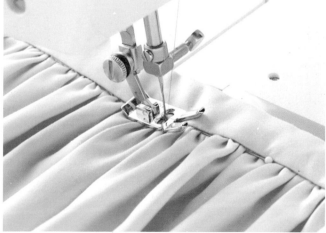

9 Attaching the band Turn the band right side out, enclosing the seam allowance on the wrong side of the skirt. From the right side of the skirt, pin the band in place, catching the lower pressed edge of the band on the wrong side.

10 Completing the vanity skirt Machine stitch from the right side, stitching just below the band but securing the band on the wrong side. Attach the skirt to the inside or outside edge of the washbasin or table.

➤ Transform an attractive side table into a practical dressing table with a boldly patterned vanity skirt. Here, the skirt is attached to the 'apron' of the table – the section just under the table top.

▲ This vanity skirt has been made using touch-and-close, gripper curtain heading tape instead of a fabric band. Stitch the heading tape along the top edge of the skirt, and gather it up as for a curtain; then stick the grip tape to the basin and hang the skirt in place.

◀ The pretty bow-print fabric of this vanity skirt links it nicely with the wallpaper.

Organza boxes

Shimmering organza, strengthened with fabric stiffener and wired seams, makes the most decorative of containers. Give them a casual, crumpled look, and scatter them with glittering trims.

Conjure up a little glamour to grace your home – these lovely boxes will add a subtle feminine touch to the bathroom. Make one to keep cotton balls within easy reach; use another for soaps, bath oils and bubble-baths; and fill another with deliciously fragrant, dried rosebuds to scent the room.

You can choose to make square or triangular boxes. The square boxes have seams threaded with fine milliner's wire, which gives surprising firmness. On the triangular box the seams are neatened with bias binding for softer support. For extra firmness, the boxes are brushed with a glue-like fabric stiffener, enabling you to scrunch the fabric into interesting shapes before the stiffener sets.

As a final flourish, decorate the box with tiny glittery beads or delicate sequins and add mini gold tassels – you can make the tassels yourself or cut them off a remnant of tassel braid.

▼ *Filmy boxes make ideal show-off containers for bathroom luxuries – your perfumed soaps, bath pearls and oils will echo the sheen and dazzle of the fabric.*

Making the square box

You can buy specially produced fabric stiffener in craft shops; you may need to water it down very slightly, so it's wise to experiment on a few samples of your fabric first. Alternatively, use PVA adhesive diluted with enough water to give it the consistency of thin cream.

On the larger boxes, the seams are wired; if you like, you can omit the base or side wiring – or both – for smaller boxes. Use milliner's wire, which is a fine, bendy wire wrapped in thread; you can buy it from florists, craft shops and some department stores.

The boxes shown here measure about 18cm (8in), 13cm (5⅛in) and 8cm (2in) square – each one is made from five fabric squares, cut 2cm (¾in) larger than the finished box size. You can make your boxes any size, but boxes over 23cm (9in) square are unlikely to hold their shape well.

You will need

- ◆ **Organza**
- ◆ **Selection of beads and sequins**
- ◆ **Gold thread for tassels (optional)**
- ◆ **Matching sewing thread**
- ◆ **Milliner's wire**
- ◆ **Fabric stiffener**
- ◆ **Small stiff brush**
- ◆ **Kitchen paper or other absorbent material**

Collect delicate sequins, tiny seed pearls, mini tassels or metallic beads and bugles to scatter in casual drifts across the crumpled organza.

1 Cutting out Decide on the finished size of the box and cut five squares of organza 2cm (¾in) larger than this.

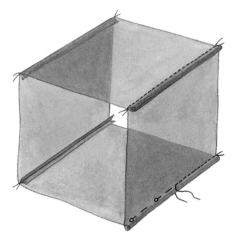

2 Joining sides with French seams With wrong sides together and taking 6mm (¼in) seam allowances, join four squares to form a loop. Trim the seam allowances to 3mm (⅛in). Fold the fabric right sides together, with the fold along one seamline; stitch again to enclose the raw edges, making a narrow French seam. Repeat with the three remaining seams.

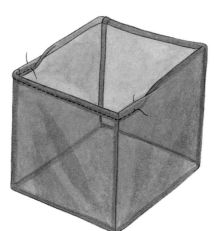

3 Adding the base To ease the corners on the lower edge, clip into the seam allowance on one side of each seam. With wrong sides together, center the lower edge of one side on one edge of the base piece; pin. Repeat all around the base. Stitch, taking 6mm (¼in) seam allowances.

5 Hemming the top edge Turn under 3mm (⅛in) then 6mm (¼in) all around the top edge; pin and stitch.

8 Applying fabric stiffener Cover the work surface with kitchen paper or other absorbent material. Then, with the box right side out, brush the fabric stiffener thinly and evenly all over it, working any excess through the fabric to the kitchen paper beneath.

9 Drying out Place the box upside down on clean newspaper to dry. When it is half dry, scrunch the fabric slightly to crumple the sides.

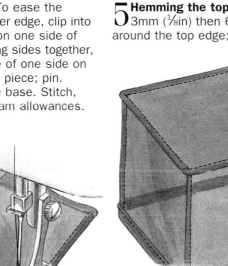

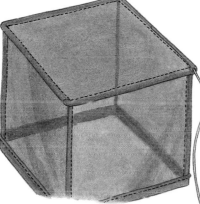

4 Completing base seam Trim the seam allowance. Complete as for the side seams in step **2** to make a French seam. At each corner, lift the needle over the side seam and pivot the fabric before continuing to stitch.

6 Wiring the base Measure around the base of the box and add 3cm (1¼in); cut a piece of wire this length. With the box wrong side out, work the end of the wire gently into the base seam at one corner and feed it along to meet the other end. Trim off and lose the end in the seam. Pinch the corners into right angles, then turn the box right side out.

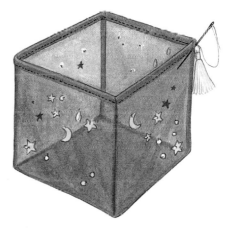

10 Decorating the box Using tiny stitches and thread to match the organza, sew on the sequins and beads, scattering them in groups over the sides. If you like, make four tassels (see below), 2.5cm (1in) long, using gold thread. Use gold thread to stitch one tassel to each outside top corner of the finished box.

7 Completing the wiring Cut four pieces of wire 1cm (⅜in) shorter than the sides. With the box right side out, wire the side seams as in step **6**. Wire the top edge as for the base.

Making a tassel

Cut a piece of card as wide as length of tassel. Wrap embroidery floss around the card about 20 times. Thread a needle with a length of floss and pass it under the loops. Remove needle and secure thread ends with a knot. Pull the loops off the card. Wrap more floss around the loops about a third of the way down. Tie the ends and tuck them inside the tassel, using a needle. Cut through bottom of loops.

Making a triangular container

This three-sided organza box has seams bound in satin bias binding, and the top edge is delicately fringed. The binding gives the seams body, so there is no need to wire them. The box shown here is about 25cm (10in) high, with 12cm (4¾in) wide sides; if you'd prefer to make a smaller box, simply cut shorter rectangles of organza in step **2**.

You will need the materials listed on page 100 – but not the wire – as well as paper, pencil and a ruler.

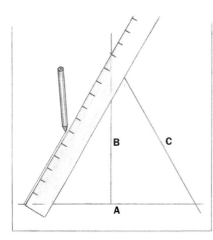

1 Making the base pattern Draw a line 12cm (4¾in) long (**A**); mark the center point. Starting at center of **A** draw a line (**B**) at right-angles to **A**. Then draw a 12cm (4¾in) long line (**C**) from one end of **A** to **B**. Repeat at the other end of **A** to form a triangle. Cut out the triangle.

2 Cutting out *For the base:* use the pattern to cut one piece from organza. *For the sides:* cut three 25 x 12cm (10 x 4¾in) rectangles.

3 Joining the sides With wrong sides together and taking a 1cm (⅜in) seam allowance, join the long edges of the rectangles to form a loop. Trim the seams to 6mm (¼in).

4 Binding the sides Topstitch the bias binding over the side seams. Turn the binding under to neaten it at the top, finishing 1cm (⅜in) from the top edge. Cut it level with the raw edges at the bottom.

5 Adding the base Ease corners on lower edge by snipping into fabric on one side of the binding at base of each side seam. Wrong sides together, center each side of the container on a base edge; pin and stitch. Trim the seam allowance to 6mm (¼in), then bind it, starting in the center of one side and mitering the corners neatly.

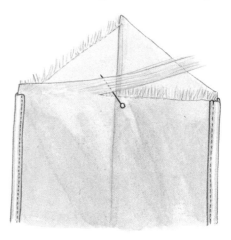

6 Fringing the top edge Using a pin, carefully tease out the horizontal threads as far as the top of the bias binding to leave a fine fringe.

7 Completing the container Apply the fabric stiffener and decorate the box as in steps **8-10** on page 101.

◀ *A tall, delicately fringed container scattered with pearl drops keeps cotton balls handy on a bathroom shelf.*

Lined laundry basket

*Turn an open wicker basket into a feature with a
fitted lining you can tie at the top with a drawstring. Choose a bright
and cheery fabric to coordinate with your bathroom.*

Tidy away all your laundry inside this neat and simple basket, smartly lined with fabric. A drawstring at the top pulls tight to hide all the unsightly soiled clothes, and narrow bows secure the lining to the sides of the basket.

It could just as well make a useful hideaway for toys in a child's play area, or for sports equipment in a teenager's room. You could store spare blankets, towels and bedlinen in it too.

For extra interest, choose a contrast color for the ties and drawstring. Here, holes have been drilled in silver-sprayed shells to trim the ends. Alternatively, you could add large beads, tassels or pompons. If you want to color co-ordinate the whole basket as in the picture, simply paint it in a matching color and then spray it with silver paint for a soft sheen.

◀▲ *With its ruffled top and decorative ties, this laundry basket lining makes a handsome contribution to the decor of the bathroom. You can leave the wicker in its natural golden state, or paint it to match your color scheme – spray paint is quick and easy to use.*

Lining the basket

Choose a washable, mediumweight fabric for the lining – crisp cottons are ideal. The sides and top of the lining are cut all in one piece, with the ties stitched into a pleat for ease. Before cutting out, decide how many ties you want – this basket has eight. The top edge is turned over and secured with two rows of stitching, making a slot for the drawstring and a deep frill above.

▲ *Crisp blue and white has a daisy-fresh appeal. The lining is easy to remove for washing or for carrying the laundry to the machine.*

You will need

- ◆ Large wicker basket
- ◆ Fabric for lining
- ◆ Fabric for ties
- ◆ Matching sewing threads
- ◆ Optional trims for drawstring
- ◆ Dressmaker's pencil
- ◆ Large safety pin or bodkin

1 Measuring up Measure from the bottom of the basket, up one side and across to the center top (**A**). Be generous to allow for contents. Measure round the top of the basket (**B**), measuring around the outside to give extra ease.

2 Cutting out For the main piece, cut a piece of fabric **A** plus 27.5cm (11in) x **B** plus 3cm (1¼in). For the base, stand the basket on the fabric and draw around it with a dressmaker's pencil; cut out.

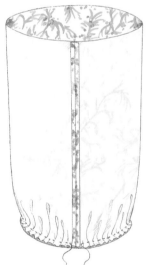

3 Seaming up Right sides together, pin and stitch side edges of main piece. Run a gathering thread around the lower edge, then divide this and the edge of the base into four. Right sides together, match marks. Draw up the gathers to fit, pin and stitch. Trim and zigzag seams.

4 Making the ties and drawstring For each tie, cut a 3 x 40cm (1¼ x 15¾in) strip. Right sides together, stitch long edges, turn out and fold in edges, slipstitching closed. For the drawstring, cut a strip 7cm (2¾in) x **B** plus 50cm (19¾in). Make up as for the ties.

5 Attaching the ties Put the lining in the basket and mark basket edge on the lining. Fold ties in half and pin in place with the fold on the line. Right sides together, fold lining along marked line over the ties; stitch 1cm (⅜in) from fold, through all layers. Unfold.

6 Making the casing At the top raw edge, turn under 1cm (⅜in), then 11cm (4¼in) and press. Stitch close to the fold, then stitch again 8cm (3¼in) from the fold. Undo the side seam between the two rows of stitching on the right side to make a slot, securing by hand at each end.

7 Finishing off Using the safety pin or bodkin, thread the drawstring through the slot, along the casing and out again. Place the lining in the basket and thread the ties through the top of the basket, tying in bows on the outside. Add trims to ends of drawstrings as desired.

Time for bed

*Ponder the delights of crisp white cotton, plumply quilted coverlets,
soft comforting blankets, downy duvets and embroidered pillows – there is a
wealth of possibilities to make your bed a haven of rest.*

A comfortable, welcoming bed after a long day is one of the pleasures of life, so deciding how you dress your bed is important. Fashions in bedding come and go: many people can remember their first encounter with a duvet or continental quilt in its crisp cotton cover – an entirely new sleeping experience. Technological developments in textiles have broadened the range of fabrics available to sleep in: the pure linen sheets of yesteryear have been superseded for many by easy-care polycotton

fabrics, while silk or satin sheets provide sheer movie-star glamour. You can smother your bed in a romance of frills and lace, or focus a sleek modern room around a duvet cover with a giant-sized contemporary screen-printed design in day-glo green.

If you resist the duvet revolution, there are plenty of other options: layer on the cosy warmth of old-fashioned blankets, create an heirloom for your family with an intricate patchwork quilt, or luxuriate under a tasseled velvet throw. In a formal, period-style

▲ *Freshly ironed white cotton sheets combined with soft camel-hair blankets and frilled cushions give an air of old-fashioned comfort. A restrained scheme of subtle caramel and beige is picked up in the checked valance and striped cushion.*

bedroom, you can tailor a cover with smart corner box pleats and piped edges, carefully coordinated to match your scheme, or add textural interest with an outline-quilted cover.

Between the sheets

The vast choice of bedlinen available today can be bewildering, but you are almost certain to find something that will not only match your scheme, but enhance the look of the room as well as providing comfort and convenience.

You can opt for a complete set, with a fitted sheet, flat sheet, pillowcases, and duvet cover, often featuring different but coordinating designs on the front and back of the duvet and pillowcases; or mix and match as you please, choosing plain sheets to tone with a strongly patterned duvet. Many ranges include a valance as well, for top-to-toe coordination, and you can easily find square continental-style pillowcases as well as the simple housewife shape or the elegant flat-bordered Oxford style.

Keeping warm

For year-round comfort while the temperature fluctuates, you can buy all-seasons duvets which split into two different thicknesses for spring and summer, or double up for extra warmth in winter. If you prefer blankets, take your pick from the luscious jewel colors in the softest wool, or cosy thermal cellular blankets in natural shades, to combine with pure white or linen sheets for a minimal, simple effect. An old-fashioned eiderdown can add just the right warmth you need, besides adding a luxurious plump look on top of the bed; alternatively, make a futon-style throw by layering batting between two pieces of fabric, and tying through at intervals with bunches of bright threads or woollen yarn.

The historic traditions and patterns of quilted bedcovers make this a very special way to add warmth, and you can record your whole family history by using scraps of familiar fabric – favorite children's clothes, a wedding dress or a celebration table cover. For a lavish look, choose a swirling, dramatic print and outline quilt it. Adding a bold border as well as beads and shells provides magical decorative detail.

▶ *Simple checks and stripes are a popular choice for bedding – they have a fresh, cheerful look and are easy to combine with other furnishings. Covered buttons or satin-stitched borders add further details.*

▲ *Vibrant with color, a bed dressed in shocking pink, scarlet and white has pillowcases printed with huge cabbage roses.*

Covering up

Many people prefer to cover the bed with a smartly cut bedcover – boxy inverted pleats at the corners, piped top edges and contrast-bound edges are all traditional, and look very much the part in a period room. This type of cover is particularly suitable for a studio or bedroom, turning the bed into a couch during the day. Add a scalloped or pointed edge for a modern look, and a couple of bolsters at each end for comfort. The top of the bed-cover can be quilted, or you could add a layer of thin batting all over and scatter with a collection of multi-colored buttons to secure the layers. For a more casual shape, a throw-over bedcover is an easy and economical option. There are plenty of Indian cotton slubby ones in earthy rich colors or natural tones – customize with a detailed trim, or add appliqué leaves or flowers swirling across for extra interest and an individual touch. For a pretty, feminine look, layer a lace bedcover or tablecloth over a colored blanket.

▼ *Blue and white marry well with traditional finishes like quilting and patchwork, keeping the fresh, clean look of a farmhouse bedroom many years ago.*

▲ *Natural linen and creamy calico make perfect partners for a crisp red and white color theme that hints at a Gallic flavor. Pile a bed with cushions covered in an easy mix of checks and stripes to reinforce the theme and welcome tired limbs.*

▼ *A severely uncluttered room in subtle neutral tones has a restful and soothing atmosphere. Simple white sheets and a natural waffle blanket have a cool, functional look without economizing on comfort.*

Dainty details

Keep the attention securely focused on the bed with tiny details that draw the eye closer. Traditional decorative effects feature all kinds of embroidery on sheets and pillows – cutwork, ribbon embroidery, drawn threadwork, cross stitch – either in plain white, cream or dainty splashes of delicate color. Try adding tiny appliquéd leaves in translucent fabrics, or a row of featherstitch in china blue on white for a classic blue room. Choose buttons and fastenings carefully – tiny corded loops and bone buttons, dainty flower shapes or opalescent pearls all heighten the feeling of care and attention to detail which make a guest feel welcome.

For a more modern effect, puncture the corners of a bedcover with eyelets and lace together with decorative cord, or add a row of huge, contrasting buttons; make up a shimmering bedcover of pale organza dotted all over with small shells; print a plain cover with your family name, or favorite poem, in gold or silver spidery script, or dot it with stenciled roses.

▲ *Simple outlines like big spots or scrolling spirals are easy to cut and appliqué to plain sheets and pillowcases for an individual and colorful twist on traditional bedlinen.*

▲ *Beautiful cutwork and scalloped edges make simple bedlinen into a luxury item. For a quick look-alike, stitch bands of openwork lace to the edges of sheets and pillowcases.*

◀ *Here simple cotton fabrics are stitched with metallic piping, fine cord loops and tiny silvery beads for unusual and subtle decoration.*

Head board styles

A sturdy head board not only makes the time you spend in bed more comfortable – it's also an important element in the room design. Choose a head-board style which will both feel good and look good.

In times gone by, a head board was an integral part of the elaborate iron, brass or wooden bedstead – though it was not always designed with comfort in mind. These days many beds come as a bed base only, without a head board, so this comfortable finishing touch is an optional extra.

There's a wide range of styles and types to choose from. It is worth thinking carefully before you choose because a head board draws the eye and can certainly form the focal point of the room. It emphasizes the position of the bed and acts as a support and backdrop to the pillows. Remember, too, that it is often flanked on either side by bedside tables and lamps – so bear these in mind when you are making your choice. Make the most of this feature when choosing a head board by selecting one that will enhance the existing

▲ *A fresh cotton print on a simple upholstered head board adds a graceful and comfortable touch to a country-style bedroom, beautifully complemented by the choice of bedlinen.*

style of the room, as well as providing you with a comfortable backrest for reading in bed, and keeping your pillows in place while you sleep.

Options

There are lots of ways in which you can provide support at the head of the bed, in keeping with your room style and budget.

Firm support

For a firm head board, carved or molded wooden boards provide the ideal touch of character for a period-style room, and they look good with a clutch of pillows piled against them. You may find a bargain in a secondhand store, while contemporary styles are sold by bed specialists.

Traditional brass or wrought iron adds period authenticity, too, while the more streamlined modern versions work well in a contemporary setting. For comfort and added detail, drape a folded throw or patchwork quilt over the top.

Simple solution

If you already have a padded head board, but it is less than inspiring or doesn't match your latest room scheme, give it a brand new cover. On a simple shape you can just smooth the new fabric over and fasten it firmly at the back with a staple gun. For more elaborate shapes, make a pull-on slip cover.

▲ *Frilly pillows and embroidered cushions, stacked against a paneled wooden head board, have all the rustic country charm of times gone by.*

▶ *Give a neat new look to an old plush head board with a simple replacement cover. Choose a substantial, closely woven fabric and even out any lumps and bumps with a layer of batting underneath. Pull the edges of the fabric firmly to the back of the head board, and staple them tightly in place. A matching valance completes the makeover.*

On a divan bed, one of the simplest and most economical solutions is to hang a covered foam squab from a decorative pole, fixed to the wall above the bed. This forms an attractive feature, with the ties and pole adding character and detail to the effect. You can also turn a divan into a seating area, by making padded boards to surround a corner – add a couple of bolsters and you have a comfortable and inviting retreat.

For a modern look, make a wrap-over cover for an MDF panel – you can button or tie it at the sides, making it easy to remove for regular laundering.

▶ *Keep the continuity by using your bedcover fabric to cover foam squabs to hang on the wall. A brass pole reflects the traditional look of this room.*

▼ *Clean square lines suit a modern room Layers of batting, covered in fabric, are wrapped over a basic sheet of MDF to create a stylish head board, held in place with discreet ties on each side.*

▲ *Bright and cheery checks and interesting angles set a young, quirky mood for this study-bedroom. Hang the panels from hooks, or fix them to the wall with Velcro strips.*

Padded boards

Nothing is more sumptuous than an upholstered head board, covered in a variety of coordinating fabrics to enhance your room scheme, and detailed with borders and delicate piping. The boards are padded with foam, then covered with batting for a beautifully smooth finish.

Many upholstered head boards feature a piped border which accentuates the shape. The border is often ruched or pleated, making it easier to cover curved edges. Some soft furnishers will make up a board to match your room, or you can upholster your own. Alternatively, for an easier option, you can buy a mail-order board that is already upholstered in calico, and add your own cover. The padding at the bottom of each example shown below is cut away, so it sits comfortably behind the mattress.

▼▶ *Mail-order upholstered head boards come in a range of shapes and styles, which you can treat in different ways (see below). Choose from rectangular (A and C), round (B) and serpentine (D). The head board (right) is a cut-away style.*

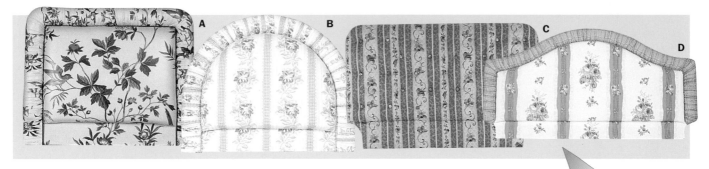

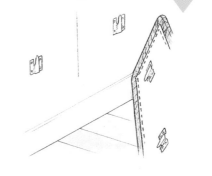

HERE'S HOW

Attaching a head board

Many beds come with two large bolts at the head end, which are designed to take a manufactured head board with slotted legs. To fix the head board in place, you just slot the legs on to the bolts, adjust the height of the board, and tighten the bolts securely.

If you are making your own head board, you can choose between two fixing options: either fix legs made from wooden battens to the board, and attach them to the bed (see Fixing with battens); or fix the head board to the wall behind the bed, using special slot plates (see Fixing to wall). You can buy slot plates at hardware stores.

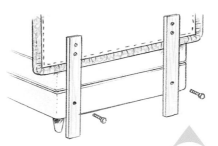

Fixing with battens You will need two 800mm (31½in) long pieces of 45 x 20mm (1¾ x ¾in) wooden batten.

With battens standing on floor against back of bed, mark bolt positions on each leg. Drill a hole at each mark; fix bolts in place temporarily. Center head board on bed, against battens. Draw around battens on back of board, then unbolt them. Drill two holes for woodscrews, spacing them equally on each batten; lay head board face down, and screw battens in place. Finally, bolt head board back on to bed.

Fixing to wall You will need two pairs of slot plates.

With head board in position, mark center top on wall. Halfway down and on either side of center point, fix one half of each pair of slot plates, tongues pointing up, and leaving screws 6mm (¼in) proud of wall. Dab chalk on screw heads. With head board in position, press it against screws, so the chalk marks it. Fix other half of plates at marks, facing downwards; drop head board on to fixings.

Duvet cover

*Make up this tailored duvet cover to give your bed a
designer look. Narrow flat piping, contrast borders and buttoned loops
add a crisply detailed but contemporary feel.*

As the bed is the focus of your bedroom, the bedlinen you choose plays an important part in the room's scheme. This is particularly true if you have a duvet rather than a bedcover – and it often proves hard to find a ready-made duvet cover to complement your chosen scheme.

Since the choice of designs in sheeting widths is narrow, this duvet set is designed to allow you to use standard width fabrics, but without unsightly seams. This way, you can coordinate your bedlinen perfectly with your color scheme. Wide borders on the sides and base of the duvet cover are crisply

picked out with flat piping in a contrast color; the opening is positioned about a third of the way down the top of the cover, breaking up the expanse of fabric, and highlighted with another contrast border. Neatly folded loops and large, eye-catching buttons give attention to detail.

Flat piping is simply a narrow fold of fabric peeping out from the seam, which adds the defining outline of ordinary piping without the extra bulk. Choose a boldly contrasting color that picks out the design of the cover.

The example shown here uses a small print for the border, and plain fabrics

▲ *The design of this duvet cover allows
you to use standard width fabric without
unsightly seams, giving you freedom to
match your scheme perfectly.*

for the rest. But you could create stunning effects using three strong plain colors – for instance, jade, blue and lilac for a cool contemporary scheme – or by using a narrow stripe for the piping. Choose interesting tortoiseshell, bone or brightly colored buttons, or for a more tailored look use self-cover buttons in one of the contrast fabrics.

Making the duvet cover

The main body of the cover is made up of three widths of 140cm (55in) wide fabric running across the width of the duvet, so bear this in mind when choosing fabric (stripes will run horizontally) and calculating quantities. This width of fabric gives enough length for a 220cm (87in) long (king size) duvet; if your duvet is smaller you can use narrower width fabric, but calculate carefully before buying. Three widths of the fabric should equal double the duvet length plus seam allowances and 16cm (6¼in) for the top panel hem.

To work out how much main fabric you need, take 28cm (11in) from the duvet width and multiply by three. All the borders for the duvet can be cut from one width of 140cm (55in) wide fabric, so you need the longest measurement of the duvet plus 2cm (¾in). Buttons are spaced about 20cm (8in) apart; you need nine for a king size. All seam allowances are 1cm (⅜in) wide.

You will need

- ◆ **140cm (55in) wide main fabric (Fabric 1)**
- ◆ **140cm (55in) wide contrast fabric for borders (Fabric 2)**
- ◆ **Contrast fabric for piping (Fabric 3)**
- ◆ **Matching thread**
- ◆ **2.5cm (1in) diameter buttons**
- ◆ **Tape measure**
- ◆ **Pins and needle**

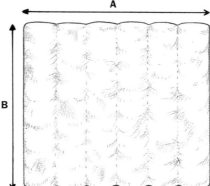

▲ *Wide borders trimmed with neat, flat piping give a crisp, smart finish to the duvet cover.*

1 Cutting the main fabric Measure the width (**A**) and the length (**B**) of the duvet. *In Fabric 1:* for the front, top and back panel, cut three pieces the fabric width by **A** less 28cm (11in) long.

2 Cutting the borders *In Fabric 2:* cut 17cm (6¾in) strips as follows: for the side borders, four pieces **B** less 13cm (5⅛in). For the bottom border, two pieces **A** plus 2cm (¾in). For the top border, two pieces **A** less 28cm (11in).

3 Preparing the flat piping *In Fabric 3:* cut enough 3cm (1¼in) strips on the straight of the grain to make four times **A** and four times **B**. Seam together to make a long strip. Wrong sides together, match long raw edges and press.

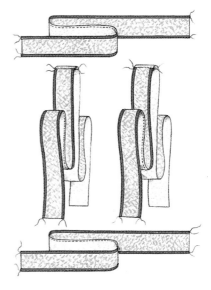

4 Piping the borders Apply the piping to the long edges of two side borders. Right sides together, pin one short edge of an unpiped border to short edge of one piped border. Neaten seams and press open. Apply piping to long edges of one bottom border and one top border piece.

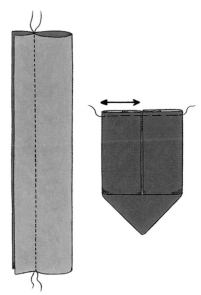

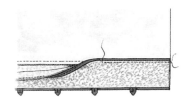

5 **Making the button loops** *In Fabric 2:* Cut a piece 5cm (2in) by 10cm (4in) for each tab. Right sides together, fold in half lengthways and stitch long raw edges. Turn out and press. Fold in half, crease and fold at a 45 degree angle to form a pointed tab. Tack across top to secure.

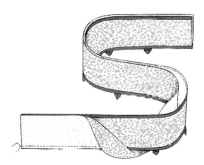

6 **Adding the loops** Allowing 1cm (⅜in) at each end, space the button loops equally on one piped edge of top border. Matching raw edges, tack in place on right side. Right sides together, and matching raw edges, pin and stitch the other top border piece to the piped edge, sandwiching loops.

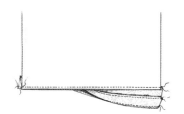

7 **Stitching the top border** Turn the top border to the right side and press. Match the right side of raw unpiped border edge to the top panel selvedge edge, wrong side; pin and stitch. Press seam towards border.

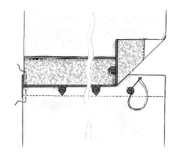

8 **Completing the top border** Bring the other piped edge of the border over, turning in seam allowances to line up with seam, and enclosing raw edges. Matching thread to border fabric, stitch 3mm (⅛in) in from piping, through all layers.

9 **Hemming the front panel** On one selvedge edge of the front panel, press under 1cm then 10cm (⅜in then 4in). Stitch close to the fold.

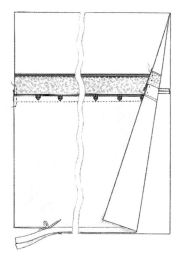

10 **Adding the buttons** Right sides up, lap the top border over the front panel by 5cm (2in), and tack together at side edges. Mark the button positions on the front panel, and stitch on.

11 **Joining the panels** Right sides together, pin and stitch the selvedge edges of the top and back panel together. Trim and neaten seam. Wrong sides together, match the front and back panels at lower edge; trim length to **B** plus 1cm (⅜in). Press top fold.

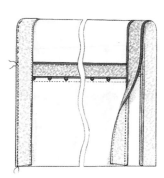

12 **Adding the side borders** Open out cover. Right sides together, pin side borders to cover, matching border seam to top fold of cover, with piped border along front edges. Trim and neaten seams; press open.

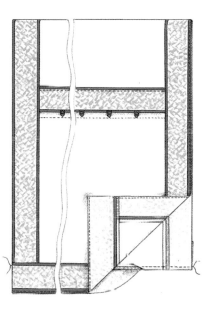

13 **Adding the bottom border** Right sides together, pin the piped bottom border to the bottom of the cover front and side borders; stitch. Repeat with unpiped border on cover back.

14 **Completing the cover** Right sides together, match outer raw edges of borders on sides and base; pin, stitch and neaten seam. Turn to right side and press.

Making flat piping from bias binding
Press open bias binding to remove crease marks. Press in half, wrong sides facing. Mark finished width of piping away from the fold and sew. Measure seam allowance from stitching to edge and trim excess.

Making the pillowcase

Matching pillowcases complete your duvet set beautifully. The pillowcase echoes the design of the duvet cover, with a wide contrast border, button loops and flat piping. The quantities given are for a standard pillow measuring 48 x 71cm (19 x 28in). For this size, you can get one case from a 140cm (55in) width of fabric. Check the size of your pillows before cutting out.

You will need

- 50cm ($^5/_8$yd) Fabric 1
- 17cm ($6^3/_4$in) Fabric 2
- Scraps of Fabric 3
- Matching thread
- Three buttons

▲ *Crisply folded button loops give interest and detail to the pillowcases.*

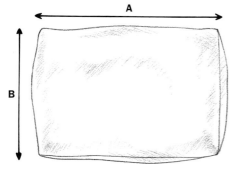

1 **Measuring and cutting** Measure the width (**A**) and the depth (**B**) of the pillow. *In Fabric 1:* cut one piece twice **A** less 2cm ($^3/_4$in). *In Fabric 2:* cut two pieces 17cm ($6^3/_4$in) by **B** plus 2cm ($^3/_4$in). *In Fabric 3:* cut two strips 3cm ($1^1/_4$in) by **B** plus 2cm ($^3/_4$in).

2 **Hemming the main fabric** On one short edge of the Fabric 1 piece, turn under a 1cm then 6cm ($^3/_8$in then $2^1/_4$in) hem. Stitch close to the fold.

3 **Adding the piping and loops** Prepare the piping as described on page 114 step **3**, and apply to both long edges of one of the border pieces. Cut out and make up three button loops as in step **5** on page 115. Space them equally on the piped border.

4 **Completing the border** Follow steps **6-8** on page 115 to attach the border to the other short edge of the main fabric piece, and to complete the border.

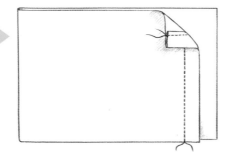

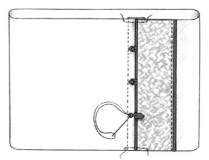

5 **Adding the buttons** Right side out, lap the looped border edge over the hemmed edge by 3cm ($1^1/_4$in); pin and tack at edges. Stitch buttons in place under the loops.

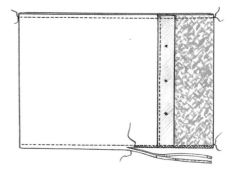

6 **Completing the pillowcase** Turn the pillowcase to the wrong side, folding at the top of the border. Pin and stitch the raw edges together; trim and neaten seam. Turn out and press.

Bluebird bedlinen

Perk up plain bedlinen with these charming appliquéd birds. Choose your own pecking order with the birds facing each other or standing in a line.

These delightful bird motifs add colorful charm to sheets. Each bird is made up of three fabric pieces – two wings and a body, appliquéd in place on the sheet or pillowcase, then finished with embroidery around the edge in soft embroidery floss. The beaks, legs and eyes are also embroidered and an outline of running stitch worked along the edge of the bedlinen completes the effect.

All you need are just three or four coordinating fabrics and a few skeins of embroidery floss. Choose small-scale unfussy fabric designs, such as gingham and small country-style prints. Pick out colors from the fabric for the embroidery floss, or choose a complementary color like the pink used around the bird's bodies here. Keep to bright orange, yellow or rust for the beak and legs to add splashes of color.

▲ *Choose fresh bold colors for the appliqué fabrics. To enhance the homespun-country appeal, you can mix small checks with mini-prints.*

Making bluebird appliqués

Full-size traceable pattern

You can work just one or a whole row of appliquéd birds along the top edge of a flat sheet. Position them all facing the same way or flip the template so some are facing away from each other. Remember to place the birds with their feet towards the top edge of the sheet so they will be the right way up when you fold the sheet back.

back wing

front wing

body

You will need

- ◆ Bedlinen to be decorated
- ◆ Odds and ends of cotton fabrics for appliqué
- ◆ Matching sewing thread
- ◆ DMC embroidery floss in pink, rust, dark blue and white, or in colors to coordinate with your fabric choice
- ◆ Tracing paper
- ◆ Pencil
- ◆ Thin card
- ◆ Dressmaker's carbon paper
- ◆ Water-soluble marker pen

1 Making the template Make a tracing of the bird, including all the shape outlines plus the beak, eye, legs and feet, and put it to one side. Then trace off the individual parts of the bird: the front wing, the back wing and the body and transfer them to the thin card. Cut them out to make templates.

2 Cutting out the shapes For each bird, use the marking pen to trace around the templates to mark a front and back wing and one body on the right side of the fabric; remember to flip the templates for birds facing the opposite direction. Mark a 6mm (¼in) seam allowance all round each shape, then cut the shapes out roughly just beyond the seam allowance.

3 Hemming the shapes Stitch around each shape just beyond the inner outline with small running stitches or machine stitching; this will help make a smooth outline. Trim each shape along outer marked line and clip into the allowance up to the stitched line at inner and outer curves. Finger press, then tack the turnings to the wrong side so the stitched line is just out of view. Group together the shapes for each bird.

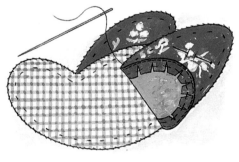

4 Stitching the birds Lay the tracing of the bird outline on the sheet in the desired position for the first bird, and secure with pins. Slip a back wing under the tracing, lining up outlines and pin in place. Remove the tracing and oversew around the edges of the back wing. Position and stitch the body and front wing in the same way. Repeat for each bird. Remove tacking stitches and pins. Lightly steam press.

5 Transferring the markings Position and pin the tracing of the bird outline over one bird. Slip a piece of dressmaker's carbon paper underneath and transfer the marking for the beak, eyes, legs and feet. Repeat for each bird.

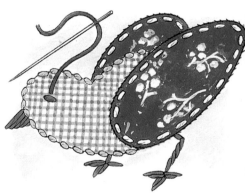

6 Embroidering the birds Using an embroidery hoop if desired, and embroidery floss, work running stitch in blue or white around the wings and oversew in pink around the body. Using the rust embroidery floss, embroider the beaks in satin stitch, legs in stem stitch and feet in straight stitch. Work a blue or white cross stitch for the eye. Work long running stitches along the machined hem at the top edge of sheet. Lightly steam press.

Velvet throw

Enjoy nights of luxury under an opulent velvet throw. The combination of large squares and triangles of shimmering pile fabrics turns a simple patchwork concept into an irresistible heirloom.

Throws are basically large pieces of fabric that you drape over beds, sofas and armchairs – but this velvet throw turns this simple concept into a sensuous luxury. Made from shimmering velvet fabrics in deep autumnal colors, and trimmed with glittering braid, fancy buttons and tassels that dangle from the corners, it is a timeless masterpiece that would give any room an instant lift – it could transform the plainest divan bed into an irresistible focal point.

For real luxury, choose velvets with a soft, silky feel. You need to source them from dress fabric departments as well as furnishing fabric suppliers. Silk velvets are ideal, but costly, and you can achieve an equally opulent look with more economical viscose versions. Experiment with different finishes – crushed, hammered and chenille velvets all give interesting, subtle effects.

Alternatively, for a more traditional room, mix crisp, floral cottons, with a heavy fringe round the outer edges. For a contemporary look, choose natural fabrics, and play with textures for a look that would have a softening effect in a contemporary, high-tech environment.

▶ *Go for truly sensuous appeal with the softest, most lustrous velvets you can buy. For adults only, this version combines deep silky reds, golds and greens, while the braid, buttons and fancy tassels underline the decadent look.*

Making the throw

At approximately 180cm (71in) square, the finished throw will fit a double bed, sofa or large armchair. It is important to cut out the squares accurately, on the straight grain of the fabric. Take 1.5cm (⅝in) seam allowances throughout. Be careful when cutting, stitching and pressing velvet.

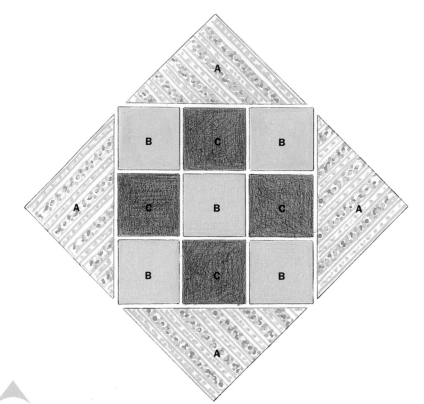

You will need

- 1.9m (2⅛yd) of 115cm (45in) wide fabric for the outer corners (A)
- 1.4m (1⅝yd) of 115cm (45in) wide fabric for central patchwork (B)
- 1m (1⅛yd) of 115cm (45in) wide contrast fabric for central patchwork (C)
- 3.7m (4⅛yd) of 115cm (45in) wide coordinating lining fabric
- 5.2m (5¾yd) braid, 4cm (1½in) wide
- Matching thread
- Four tassels
- Four 4cm (1½in) buttons
- Even-feed sewing machine foot (optional)

1 Cutting out the patchwork *From fabric **A**:* cut two 93cm (36¾in) squares. Fold each square in half diagonally, then cut across the diagonal fold to make four triangles, each with two sides measuring 93cm (36¾in). *From fabric **B**:* cut five 45cm (17¾in) squares. *From fabric **C**:* cut four 45cm (17¾in) squares.

2 Cutting out the lining Cut the lining fabric in half widthways, to make two pieces approximately 185 x 115cm (73¼ x 45in). Put one piece aside for lining the center panel. From the other piece, cut two 185 x 37cm (73¼ x 14½in) pieces for the outer lining strips.

3 Arranging the central squares Following the diagram above left, arrange the central patchwork squares in three rows of three. If you are using velvet, make sure that the pile is running in the desired direction on each square.

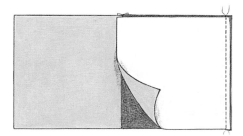

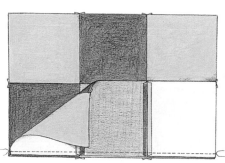

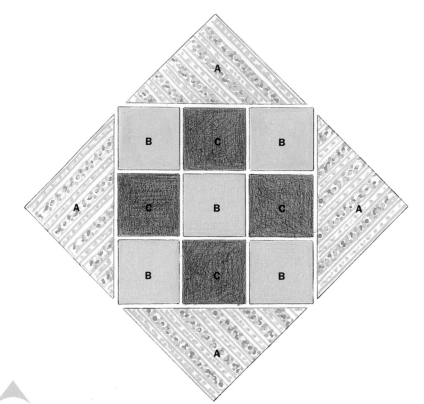

4 Stitching the strips If you wish, fit an even-feed foot to your sewing machine. With right sides together and raw edges level, pin and stitch the patches in the correct order in strips of three. Press the seams open, working from the wrong side; if you are pressing velvet, use a needleboard or a scrap of self-fabric to protect the pile from being crushed.

5 Joining the strips together With right sides together and seams level, pin and stitch the patchwork strips together, making sure that they are in the right order. Press the seams open, as in step **4**.

6 Marking the edges Using pins, mark the center point of each edge of the patchwork square. Repeat to mark the center point of the long edge of each fabric triangle.

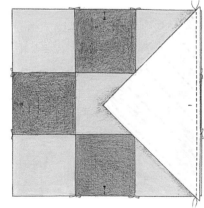

7 Adding the triangles With right sides together, raw edges level and center points matching, pin the long edge of a fabric triangle to one side edge of the patchwork. Tack and stitch in place, working with the triangle uppermost and checking that it does not pucker. Repeat to stitch the remaining three triangles in place.

8 Adding the braid With right sides uppermost, pin, then tack the braid centrally over the seam joining one triangle to the center patchwork. Stitch each long edge, working in the same direction to avoid puckers. Repeat to stitch braid over the other three triangle seams, overlapping the ends where they meet.

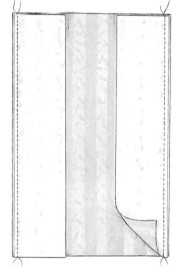

9 Preparing the lining With right sides together and raw edges level, pin, then stitch one outer lining strip to each long edge of the main lining panel. Press the seams open.

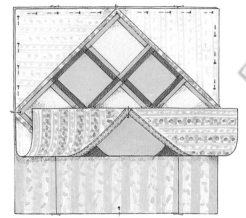

10 Pinning lining Use pins to mark the center of each edge of the throw and lining. Lay lining flat, right side up. Pin the throw on top, right side down, matching center edges. If edges of throw and lining do not match exactly, pin together so layers lie flat, then trim away any excess.

11 Stitching lining Tack, then stitch all around, leaving a 25cm (10in) gap along one edge, away from braid. Trim corners and turn right side out through the gap. Tuck in raw edges along opening and slipstitch closed.

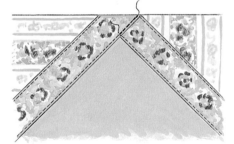

12 Securing the seams Starting at one edge, and working from the right side, machine stitch along one row of braid stitching for about 2.5cm (1in) in to help the seam lie flat. Repeat at each edge.

13 Completing the throw Stitch a button at each corner of center square. Stitch a tassel to each outer corner of throw, securing the threads between lining and right side of throw.

◄ *Different fabrics give a variety of effects. For a traditional look, mix crisp, floral cottons, or use natural, textured fabrics for a more modern feel. For a really funky look, jazz up a room with a combination of animal prints and fur fabrics.*

Fabric clothes covers

*Zip-up fabric covers are a practical and pretty
way to keep clothes clean and tidy, whether they're
in daily use or for seasonal storage.*

*The covers are good for
protecting clothes hung
on open rails or pegs,
and in conventional
wardrobes. They also
make excellent travel
bags for suits, dresses
and skirts.*

Clothes stored for any length of time, even when they are hanging in a wardrobe, can soon become dusty and creased. The best way to keep them fresh and wrinkle-free is to seal them in protective bags.

Fabric clothes covers have a major advantage over the plastic covers sold in department stores. Unlike plastic, fabric is porous and allows air to circulate around the garments, keeping them aired and preventing the growth of

unpleasant fabric molds, such as mildew. Making your own covers means you can match them with linking accessories, such as padded coathangers and lavender-scented sachets to keep moths at bay.

Instructions are given for two styles of cover – one with a gusset and the other without. Both have a shaped top edge, an opening at the top for the clothes hanger hook, and long zip-up openings, so that you can get at the clothes easily.

Short cover with gusset

The steps below are for a short cover with a gusset. The finished measurements are about 97 x 56 x 7cm (38¼ x 22¼ x 2¾in), which makes it ideal for jackets, shirts, blouses and short dresses. If you wish to make a longer cover, for a long dress say, you will need to buy extra fabric and cut longer pieces.

Closely woven furnishing cotton is the best choice of fabric for the bag, as it is sturdy and durable, but you could also use a firmly woven dress cotton. You can buy zippers by the meter (yard) from fabric stores, in a limited range of colors. Unless otherwise stated, take 1.5cm (⅝in) seams throughout

You will need

- ◆ **1.5m (1⅝yd) of 140cm (55in) wide fabric**
- ◆ **1m (1⅛yd) of zipper by the meter (yard) plus one zipper pull**
- ◆ **6.5m (7⅛yd) of matching bias binding**
- ◆ **Matching sewing threads**
- ◆ **Paper (optional)**
- ◆ **Pencil**
- ◆ **Scissors**

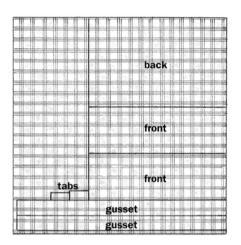

1 Cutting out the cover *For the back:* cut one rectangle 100 x 58cm (39½ x 23in). *For the fronts:* cut two rectangles 100 x 30.5cm (39½ x 12in). *For the gusset:* cut two rectangles 146 x 10cm (57⅜ x 4in). *For top tab:* cut a 12 x 5.5cm (4¾ x 2⅛in) strip. *For the bottom tab:* cut one 14 x 6cm (5½ x 2½in) strip.

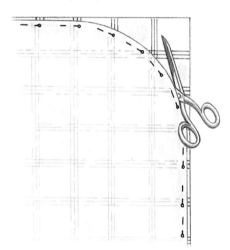

2 Shaping the top curve Lay one front rectangle out flat. Starting at one corner, measure and mark 16cm (6¼in) along short edge and 16cm (6¼in) down adjoining long edge. Join the two points with a smooth curve and cut along the curve. Right sides together, use the shaped front to cut the same shaping on other front. Then fold back rectangle in half widthways and use one front rectangle as a pattern to shape the top corners.

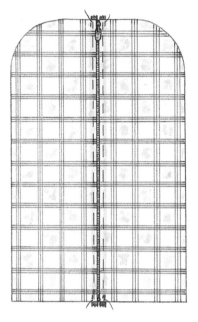

3 Inserting zipper On long, straight edge of each front piece, press under 1.5cm (⅝in). Slip zipper pull on one end of zipper. Insert zipper, matching pressed edges of fronts with outer edges of zipper teeth, and stitching 6mm (¼in) from folded edges.

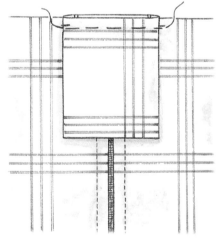

4 Making and attaching top tab Pin the top tab in half widthways and stitch both long edges, taking 1.2cm (½in) seams. Trim the seams and clip the corners at the folded edge. Turn to the right side and press. With the raw edges matching, center the tab at the top front of the bag; tack in place.

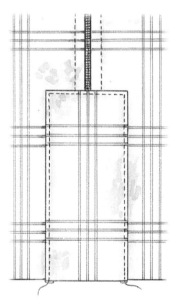

5 Making bottom tab Press under 1.5cm (⅝in) on both long edges and one short edge of the bottom tab and tack in place. Center tab at lower edge of bag front, matching the raw edges; tack. Stitch close to the three folded edges of the tab.

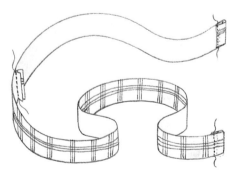

6 Preparing the gusset Press under 6mm (¼in), then 1cm (⅜in) on one short end of each gusset strip; stitch. With right sides together, tack the short raw edges together.

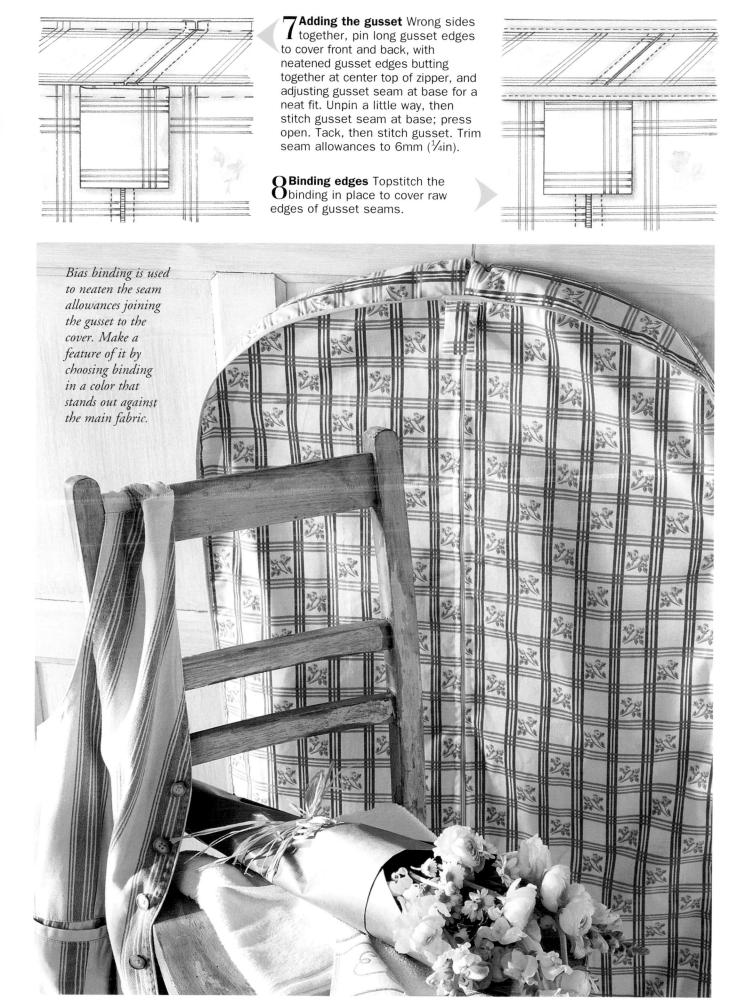

7 Adding the gusset Wrong sides together, pin long gusset edges to cover front and back, with neatened gusset edges butting together at center top of zipper, and adjusting gusset seam at base for a neat fit. Unpin a little way, then stitch gusset seam at base; press open. Tack, then stitch gusset. Trim seam allowances to 6mm (¼in).

8 Binding edges Topstitch the binding in place to cover raw edges of gusset seams.

Bias binding is used to neaten the seam allowances joining the gusset to the cover. Make a feature of it by choosing binding in a color that stands out against the main fabric.

Long cover without gusset

This easy variation of the short clothes cover has no gusset. It is ideal for lightweight garments, such as trousers, blouses, dresses and long summer skirts.

The instructions below are for a cover measuring about 147 x 57cm (57 x 22¼in). It will take a dress up to about 145cm (56in) long. If the bag is for a particular dress, measure the length and cut the bag to the required length, adding an extra 3cm (1¼in) for seam allowances. Buy a longer zipper and add any extra length on to the fabric requirements.

You will need

- ◆ **1.5m (⁵⁄₈yd) of 140cm (55in) wide fabric**
- ◆ **1.5m (1⁵⁄₈yd) of zipper by the meter (yard) plus one zipper pull**
- ◆ **4.5m (5yd) of matching bias binding**
- ◆ **Matching sewing threads**
- ◆ **Paper (optional)**
- ◆ **Pencil and scissors**

1 Cutting out the cover
For the back: cut one rectangle 1.5m x 60cm (59 x 23½in).
For the fronts: cut two 1.5m x 31.5cm (59 x 12⅜in) rectangles.
For the bottom tab: cut one strip 14 x 6cm (5½ x 2½in).
For the top tab: cut one strip 12 x 5.5cm (4¾ x 2½in).

2 Preparing the front
Follow steps **2-5** on page 124 to shape the top edges of the cover, insert the zipper and attach the top and bottom tabs.

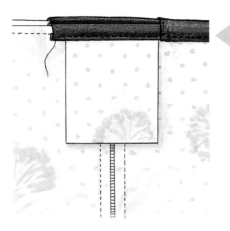

3 Neatening hook area
Cut two 5cm (2in) strips of bias binding and press in half lengthways. Fold one piece centrally over the raw edges of top tab and front cover section; pin, tack and stitch. Repeat to stitch the other length over the raw edge of the back cover piece, matching the center of the bias binding to the center top edge of the back; stitch.

4 Assembling bag With wrong sides together, place the two bag sections together. Pin, tack and stitch round all raw edges, but do not stitch across the top tab. Trim the seam allowances to 6mm (¼in). Bind the seam allowances as in step **8** on page 125, overlapping the raw ends of the binding at the center top.

5 Reinforcing opening Cut two 3cm (1¼in) pieces of binding. Press under 6mm (¼in) on each short end. Fold one piece over bound edge either side of top tab; slipstitch in place.

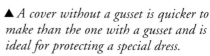

▲ *A cover without a gusset is quicker to make than the one with a gusset and is ideal for protecting a special dress.*

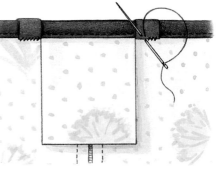

Tented wardrobe

*Solve your storage problems stylishly with a fabric-covered
wardrobe. It's a clever way to welcome a guest to a spare room
and can be stored away at other times.*

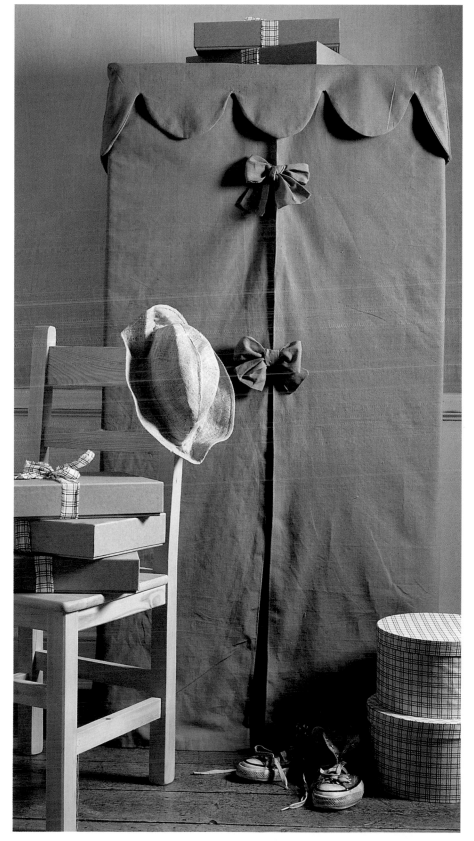

With space at a premium in most homes, flexible, temporary storage with good looks is always welcome. Most people have guests from time to time, but the spare room usually fulfils several other roles in between, so a wardrobe may take space you can't afford. An attractive, fabric-covered wardrobe that you can easily put up and take down is the perfect answer.

Choose fabrics carefully to complement the room scheme. Make a wardrobe covered in billowing roses for a country feel; broad military stripes and a rich fringe have a period campaign look; or go theatrical with rich colors and grand tassels.

You will probably find lots of other uses too: a tented wardrobe is fun for a child's room, where it can also be used as a play tent. Choose cheery checks and jazzy character prints to create a fun feel. Provide budget-conscious and decorative hanging storage for a studio room, or use it to store out of season clothing in a spare room.

You can buy tented wardrobe frames from large department stores or by mail order. They come in two different shapes – with either a flat or sloping top. Some wardrobes come with a basic cover, but making a new one is straightforward and inexpensive.

A decorative pelmet gives you extra design potential – choose the shape to suit your room and fabric. Scallop trims give a feminine look, zigzag points lend a child's room a circus feel, and gothic points add drama to a period style.

◀ *A fabric cover with bows and a
scalloped pelmet transforms a wardrobe
frame into a decorative and functional
feature of the room.*

Making a tented wardrobe

These instructions are for a free-standing, flat-topped wardrobe, with a shaped pelmet and ties to secure the front opening. The front opening edges are strengthened with interfacing, but select a firm fabric with plenty of body for best results. A contrasting fabric for the pelmet and ties adds to the decorative impact: you can use an inexpensive plain cotton for the main wardrobe, with a matching print for the pelmet.

Before buying your fabric, erect the wardrobe frame and measure up as in step **1** right, to work out how much you need. The side and front sections are cut in one piece. If you use a 137cm (54in) wide fabric without nap, you can cut the pelmet lengthways alongside the main pieces, so you need the wardrobe height x 3, plus the depth (for the top section). For directional (stripes, for example) or narrower fabrics add extra for cutting the pelmet across the width. As the wardrobe is usually placed against a wall, you can leave the back of the pelmet straight.

You will need

- ◆ **Flat-topped wardrobe frame**
- ◆ **Furnishing fabric**
- ◆ **Contrast for pelmet (optional)**
- ◆ **Matching thread**
- ◆ **Mediumweight iron-on interfacing**
- ◆ **Tape measure**
- ◆ **Paper for pelmet pattern**
- ◆ **Dressmaker's pencil**
- ◆ **Iron**

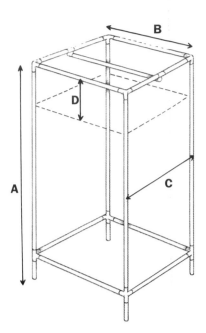

1 Measuring up Measure height (**A**) and add 7.5cm (3in). Measure width (**B**), and depth (**C**). Add 1cm ($\frac{3}{8}$in) to **B** + **C** for ease. Decide on pelmet depth (**D**) – about 18cm (7in).

Once the top piece has been stitched on, fit the cover over the frame and pin it up at the bottom to check the length before hemming.

2 Cutting the main pieces *For the back*, cut one piece **A** x **B** plus 3cm (1¼in). For the side fronts, add half of **B** to **C**, plus 14.5cm (5¾in) for facings and seams. Cut two pieces this width x **A**. For the top, add 3cm (1¼in) to both **B** and **C** and cut one piece to this size.

3 Cutting the pelmet strips *For the total pelmet width*, add **B** and **C** together, multiply by 2 and add 3cm (1¼in). Cut two pieces this measurement by **D** plus 3cm (1¼in), or enough widths to make up the total pelmet width twice. Join widths if necessary, pressing seams open.

4 **Interfacing the front edges** Cut two pieces of interfacing **A** x 13cm (5⅛in). On the wrong side of one long edge of each side front, position the interfacing strip 6mm (¼in) in, and fuse. Press the hem allowance over the interfacing, and stitch down. Press the facing to the wrong side.

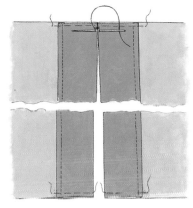

5 **Joining the front edges** Tack the facing in place at the top and bottom edges. Align the two front edges, and oversew together firmly with doubled thread to 2.5cm (1in) from the top.

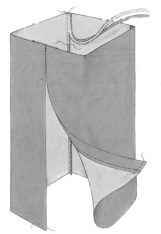

6 **Joining the back seams** Right sides together, pin the side front edges to each side of the back section, and stitch. Trim the seam and neaten with zigzag stitch.

7 **Cutting the pelmet pattern** Cut a piece of paper measuring **C** x 2 plus **B**, by the pelmet depth plus 3cm (1¼in). Fold in half widthways to find the center front, and mark in the front corners, half the width of **B** from the fold.

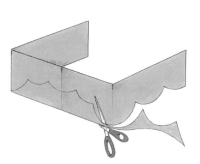

8 **Shaping the pattern** Draw in your chosen shaping for the front and sides of the pelmet. Here, three scallops run across the front of the wardrobe, swooping to deeper scallops around the front corners and along the sides. Cut out the shape.

9 **Cutting the pelmet shape** Right sides together, fold the pelmet strips in half widthways, to mark the center. Open out, and center the pattern on top. Pin and cut around the pattern through both layers, marking in the corners.

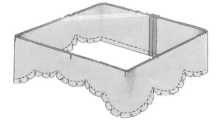

10 **Stitching the pelmet** Join the ends of each strip to form a loop, and press seams open. Right sides together, pin and stitch the lower edges together, trimming and clipping the seam allowances as necessary. Turn to right side and press.

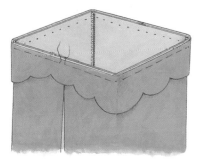

11 **Attaching the pelmet** With the pelmet facing and the right side of the main sections together, match the top edges, center fronts and front corners. Tack all around the top edge.

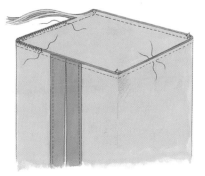

12 **Adding the top** Turn the wardrobe wrong side out. Right sides together, pin the top piece to the top edges of the wardrobe, sandwiching the pelmet, and matching center front and corner marks. Stitch through all layers. Trim seam, layering to reduce bulk, and clip corners. Zigzag stitch to neaten.

13 **Hemming the bottom edge** Fit the cover over the wardrobe frame, and pin up the hem at floor level. Remove the cover. Turn under 1cm (⅜in) at the raw edge, and machine or slipstitch the hem in place.

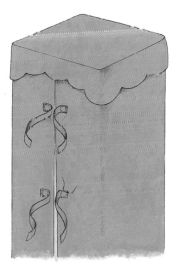

14 **Making the ties** Cut four strips 35 x 8cm (13¾ x 3¼in). Fold each strip in half along its length, and stitch the long edge and one short edge, taking a 1.5cm (⅝in) seam. Turn out, press and slipstitch end closed.

15 **Stitching on the ties** Pin the ends of the ties in position opposite each other on the front edges, placing one pair 30cm (12in) down from the top and the other 50cm (19¾in) below them. Stitch in a square to secure.

Gable-topped wardrobe

Some tented wardrobes have sloping gabled tops, dramatically increasing the tent effect. Make the most of the shape by adding a pennant-shaped pelmet or curvy petal points. The main construction of the wardrobe is the same as for the tented wardrobe, except that the roof rises steeply over two triangles to make the gable ends.

You will need

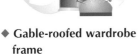

◆ **Gable-roofed wardrobe frame**

◆ **Furnishing fabric**

◆ **Contrast for pelmet (optional)**

◆ **Matching thread**

◆ **Mediumweight iron-on interfacing**

◆ **Tape measure**

◆ **Paper for gable pattern**

◆ **Dressmaker's pencil**

◆ **Iron**

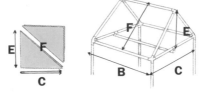

1 Making the roof pattern Measure up as in step **1** on page 128. For gable ends, measure the roof height (**E**) and cut a piece of paper **E** by **C**. Fold in half across the width and draw a line (**F**) from the top of the fold to the outer corner. Cut along the line and open out.

2 Cutting out Cut all the main pieces as in step **2** on page 128 except the top piece. Adding 1.5cm (⅝in) all around, cut two pieces from the gable pattern. For the roof piece, cut a piece **F** x 2 plus 3cm (1¼in), by **B** plus 3cm (1¼in), and clip the seam allowance at the center point on each edge.

3 Making up the wardrobe Continue through steps **3-11** on pages 128–129 to make up the main sections and pelmet.

▼ *Match the color and pattern of the wardrobe cover to the decor for a bed-cum-playroom every child will long for.*

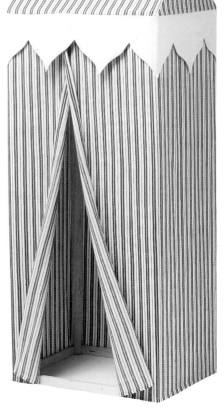

▲ *Stripy fabric, coupled with bold petal points, gives the effect of a mini-marquee.*

4 Stitching the roof sections Right sides together, match the center clips on the roof piece with the top point of each triangle, and continue pinning down the sides. Stitch both seams, trim and zigzag to neaten.

5 Finishing the wardrobe Complete as in steps **12-15** on page 129.

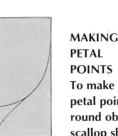

Tip

MAKING PETAL POINTS
To make a template for petal points, use a round object to draw a scallop shape, about two thirds of the total finished depth. Fold down the center, and extend the line of the scallop to the bottom of the fold to make the point. Trim along the line and open out.

Voile chair cover

*Dotted voile makes a delicate covering for a plain chair; piping
and a padded seat give extra substance, with rosebuds to fasten
the back – echoing the same theme as the cushion.*

You can make this slipover cover for any chair without arms, with either a straight or a curved back, using a pattern tailor-made for your own chair. If the back struts of the chair are particularly thick, however, the cover may not be suitable as it does not have a back gusset. Use a fine fabric to make the cover, such as voile or organza. You can find suitable fabrics in both soft furnishing and dress fabric departments, though fabric sold for curtaining is likely to be more durable.

Make the pattern up first in paper, then calculate the amount of fabric you need to buy for the chair.

◀▲ *Make the most of the pretty printed voiles available to soften the outlines of a plain old bedroom chair, and give it a fresh and graceful air.*

Making the chair cover

The chair cover has a comfortable padded seat and for this you need heavyweight batting. You also need piping cord; buy enough to go all the way around the seat and up both sides and across the top of the back. Newspaper is ideal to make the pattern.

1 Shaping the seat and back Lay a piece of paper on the seat and draw a line around the edge; cut out. For the back, tape another piece of paper from top of chair back to seat, meeting edge to edge with the seat pattern at the bottom. Trim sides and top edges so they wrap halfway round the thickness of the back.

2 Cutting the back panel Cut a piece of paper for the back panel. Trim the sides and top to meet the front pattern, and follow the line of the back legs to the floor. Trim the bottom edge straight.

3 Cutting the skirt pattern Tape a piece of paper around the seat edge with the top edge meeting the edge of seat pattern and the side edges level with back panel. Butt it up to the back pattern on the back legs, and mark the front corners at the top edge.

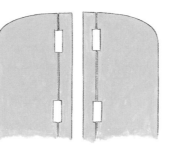

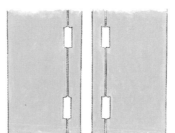

4 Preparing the pattern Remove the pattern from the chair. To add fullness at each leg, cut through the skirt pattern at each corner from top to bottom and add a paper panel 7.5cm (3in) wide at each corner and side edge. For the back overlap, fold the back panel in half down its length and cut along the fold. Add a 5cm (2in) strip to the fold edge of each section.

5 Cutting the fabric Lay out the pattern on the fabric, adding 1.5cm (⅝in) seam allowances, and 2cm (¾in) on the bottom edges for hems. For piping, cut enough 4cm (1½in) wide bias strips to go all around the seat, up both sides and over top of back. On skirt, mark in the centers of the front gathering panels.

You will need

- ◆ **Fabric for chair cover**
- ◆ **Piping cord, size 4**
- ◆ **8oz (200g) heavyweight batting**
- ◆ **Lining fabric for seat pad**
- ◆ **Two Velcro spots**
- ◆ **Paper for pattern**

6 Adding the piping Make up piping and apply it round seat edge and round the top and sides of the back piece. Right sides together, pin and stitch the seat and back pieces together along back edge of the seat.

7 Gathering the skirt On the skirt, measure and mark 7.5cm (3in) on either side of the marked front corner points. Run two rows of gathering stitches along the top of each marked section. Excluding the seam allowance, gather 15cm (6in) at each end of the skirt in the same way.

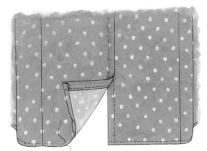

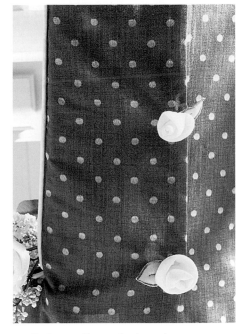

8 Joining the seat and skirt Pull up the gathering threads to measure 7.5cm (3in), and fasten temporarily by winding around a pin. Right sides together, pin the skirt to the seat, matching the corner points, leaving the end seam allowances free. Adjust the gathers if necessary. Stitch.

11 Turning up the hem Fit the cover on the chair and trim the bottom edge straight. First, press under 1cm (⅜in) then another 1cm (⅜in). Pin in place and stitch.

12 Padding the seat From the seat pattern, cut two pieces in batting and one in lining, adding 1cm (⅜in) all around each piece. Pin and tack the batting to the wrong side of the main voile seat section.

▲ *Dainty voile rosebuds make an unusual and attractive back detail, concealing practical Velcro fastenings.*

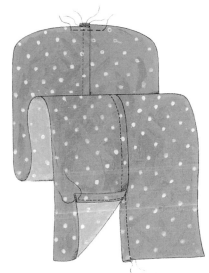

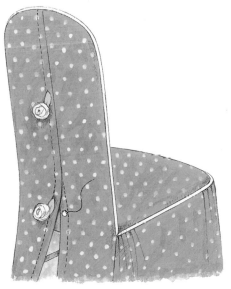

9 Finishing the back opening On the long edge of each back panel, press under 1cm (⅜in) then 2.5cm (1in). Stitch close to the inner fold. Right side up, lay the two pieces side by side and lap the left over the right by 2.5cm (1in). Tack across the top.

13 Lining the seat Folding the skirt and back into the middle of the seat, pin the lining to the seat, right sides together. Stitch, leaving a 10cm (4in) gap. Turn through and slipstitch closed.

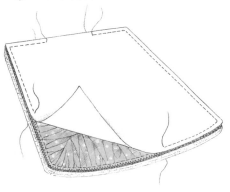

14 Finishing off Make up two rosebuds and two leaves (see below) and stitch each leaf to a rosebud. Stitch the rosebuds on the left side of the overlap, one level with the seat and one halfway up the seat back. Stitch Velcro spots under each rosebud and on corresponding positions on underlap to fasten.

10 Adding the back panel Right sides together, match the edges of the front back piece and the back panel and pin. Continue down the side edges of the back panel, pinning it to the skirt. Stitch. Trim all seams and zigzag to neaten.

Making a rosebud Fold a 30 x 8cm (12 x 3¼in) voile strip in half lengthways around batting and trim curves at each end. Using double thread, stitch 6mm (¼in) from the edge and loosely gather. Roll up three turns tightly and stitch through to secure. Roll the rest less tightly, pulling the gathers. Stitch through the base to secure as you go and work a few firm backstitches when rolled. Cut out two fabric leaves. Stitch them together around a layer of batting, using close satin stitch. Stitch around the edges and along center of leaf.

Making the embroidered cushion

An embroidered rose makes a pretty centerpiece for a cushion, framed with a toning fabric. This stylized design is quick to complete in outline stitch and satin stitch. Exact thread colors are given here, but to match a different color scheme, choose two shades of one color for the inner and outer rose petals, and two shades of a neutral color to outline them; the darker outline color is also used to outline the green of the leaves. Narrow linen tape covers the raw edge of the fabric and makes a subtle frame for the embroidery here, but you could use a ribbon or braid instead. Pompons cut from a bobble braid add dainty detail at the corners.

You will need

- ◆ 30cm (⅓yd) fabric for cover
- ◆ 25cm (10in) square of fabric for embroidery
- ◆ DMC floss, one skein each of 305, 292, 889, 887 and 876
- ◆ 28-30cm (11-12in) cushion pad
- ◆ Dressmaker's carbon paper
- ◆ Crewel needle, size 9
- ◆ Tracing paper and pencil
- ◆ Embroidery hoop
- ◆ 1.1m (1¼yd) of narrow linen tape
- ◆ 4 pompons

▶ *A simple piece of hand embroidery turns a plain cushion into something special.*

Full-size traceable pattern

1 Transferring the motif Trace and transfer the rose motif to the center of the square of fabric.

2 Working the satin stitch Fit the fabric into the embroidery hoop. Working in satin stitch, and using two strands of floss, fill in the center sections of the rose in 305, the outer petals in 292, and the leaves in 876.

3 Outlining the shapes Working in outline stitch with two strands of floss, outline the inner petals of the rose in 889, the outer ones in 887, and the leaves in 889.

4 Cutting the cushion From the main fabric, cut one 30cm (12in) square and one piece 30cm (12in) deep by 40cm (15¾in). Cut this piece in half vertically.

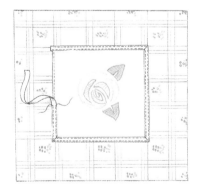

5 Applying the embroidery Center the embroidery on the front of the cushion and tack in place. Starting in one corner, pin the tape over the raw edge, mitering the corners and tucking the last end under the miter, as described on page 55 in steps **3** and **4**.

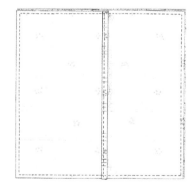

6 Completing the cushion On the cut edges of the back halves, press under and stitch a double 1cm (⅜in) hem. Overlap the two sides by 2.5cm (1in) and pin. Pin back and front right sides together and stitch all around; neaten and turn out. Stitch a bobble at each corner.

Nursery fabrics

*Fabrics designed to delight young eyes provide a kaleidoscope
of color and inspiration in the nursery. From Mickey Mouse to
Treasure Island, cheerful designs make bedtime fun.*

No one child is the same as the next, so it's just as well that designers are very aware of the discerning eye and distinct ideas of the younger generation. To satisfy this market, there is a flood of specially designed fabrics and wallcoverings to make the room of your child's dreams.

You can introduce a pattern in one item – perhaps a huge cushion in a big print of dancing teddies – or coordinate a whole room with a range of matching and toning fabrics, featuring an eye-catching cartoon character or loveable animal set against brisk checks, dotty designs, simple miniprints, and plains.

Plump for the sizzling primary colors that so many children are drawn to – bright red, electric blue and canary yellow. Indulge a little girl's fancy with pretty pastels; or provide a varied palette of tropical brights or the subtle hues of woodland creatures.

Learning to appreciate color, shape

▲ *For a room that grows with your child, base the scheme round a bold print, and use abstracts for accessories like cushions and bags that you can change as your child grows.*

and pattern is an important part of every child's early development. You can use the opportunity of decorating and furnishing the room to surround your child with lots of absorbing and satisfying visual stimulation.

Using nursery fabrics

If you are decorating a room from scratch, it is best to choose your main fabric first and let the design of the fabric suggest the way you use it. For example, you may choose a print which has huge cartoon characters. Large-scale prints like this are often best displayed over a large area – in the form of long curtains, say, or made up as a duvet cover. On the other hand, a fabric with a detailed figurative border would work particularly well on the lower edge of a blind, or as an edging for plain curtains.

You can make an expensive fabric go a long way by making it up into a patch-work quilt, combined with cheaper toning prints and plains, or by cutting out the individual motifs to appliqué on to plain curtains and cushions cut from more economical fabric ranges.

Choose from a wide variety of themes – you'll find that they will inspire you to accessorize the room to match. Curtains scattered with somersaulting clowns, for example, look wonderful topped with a pennant pelmet finished with tinkling bells and ribbons. A print of lions and tigers demands a cuddly throw of fur fabric for the bed; or you could create grinning cat cushions to coordinate with a fabric covered with kittens.

▲ *Go to the circus with clowns, performing animals and big top pennants, all inspired by the print on the duvet and crib bumper.*

◄ *Encourage tidy habits with softly padded hanging pockets cut to imitate brightly colored plant pots. Decorate with giant flowers and use to store little treasures.*

Abstract designs

If you want to design a room which will look good both now and in the longer term, you need to find a basic style which will really grow with your child. Look out for prints that are designed to please children of all ages, rather than those that are restricted to a particular stage of childhood.

Choose fabrics that concentrate on color and pattern rather than specific characters. Children love jazzy abstract prints based on tribal designs, spotty or swirly designs, bright checks and stripes, or harlequin patterns in strong pastels. Use a mixture for extra interest, and add more specific references to your child's age in smaller accessories – such as scatter cushions, useful drawstring bags, framed fabric pictures, and hanging pockets, which you can change and adapt as your child grows.

▲ *Indulge your little girl's fancy with a room that's fit for a princess, yet still practical. Here, a crisp candy striped fabric is made into a romantic bed drape and a handy drawstring bag. The bedlinen and curtains use a mix of pink and white prints, highlighting a charming wallpaper border.*

▼ *A bold teddy bear print in warm pastels is a classic choice for a nursery window. The flat curtains make the most of the comforting motif, while starry tab buttons and the coordinating blind and wallpaper add small-scale detail.*

HERE'S HOW

Embellishing bedlinen

Turn plain bedlinen into a child-friendly feature with quick no-sew appliqué. Cut out your child's favorite motifs from a fabric print – such as scraps left over from a quilt cover or curtains – and arrange them on a plain pillowcase and duvet or sheet. Fuse the the motifs in place using WonderUnder, as described on page 74. Outline the shapes with dimensional paints (puff paints) for added emphasis but make sure you buy the washable sort.

Animal magic

The endlessly varied inhabitants of the animal kingdom hold an enduring fascination for children of all ages, and make an ideal subject for a theme for children's rooms. Classic characters, such as cuddly farmyard animals and Beatrix Potter's rabbits, ducks and mice; cartoon personalities like Bambi or the Lion King; wild animals from exotic places, tiny little door mice or jolly trunk-waving elephants – you will find them all, pictured in glowing color, on a panorama of fabrics in most stores. As the colors are often quite strong, you can base the whole room scheme on one fabric, picking latex or acrylic paint and gloss paint to match, and echoing the theme – rabbits, perhaps, or zoo creatures – in lamps, pictures and toys. Many of the coordinated ranges have wallpaper and borders to match, to surround your child with fun and interest.

▶ *The chickens on the roller blind inspired the handpainted wall border, while color-matched spots, stripes, checks and a miniprint provide a cheerful foil on the pennant-shaped pelmet, bed and pleated lampshade.*

▼ *There's a huge choice of decorative details with an animal theme, like this frog finial, that will appeal to your child's sense of fun.*

▼ *Two fabric motifs, cut from a bold animal print, inspired this matched pair of green and white gingham pajama cases. The motifs are secured with machine zigzag stitch.*

Nursery wallhanging

Soft, fabric pictures make wonderful child-friendly decorations for your baby's nursery. This one has lots of colorful padded appliqué designs and pockets to hold tiny toys.

Young children will love identifying the motifs on this lively wallhanging. And as they get older they will love using the pockets to keep their treasures safe.

A colorful wallhanging is a delightful finishing touch for a baby's nursery. This one has a plain fabric background with a patterned border, but you could use four different fabrics, one for each border strip. If you have made a quilt or curtains for the nursery, use any left-over fabric for the borders for a coordinated look.

The appliqué motifs use lots of different patterned fabrics, so if you plan to make the wallhanging, start saving all your scraps or look out for inexpensive remnants. You can copy this design exactly by using the templates on pages 143 and 144, or adapt the designs to make the best use of the fabrics you already have, or to introduce different motifs – your child's favorite animal or toy, for example.

Some of the designs are padded with washable polyester batting for a three-dimensional effect; others are flat and some, such as the house, tractor and basket shapes, are sewn as pockets. A little simple embroidery is used to complete the designs.

Making the wallhanging

The wallhanging has a front and a back both made exactly the same with a border. Prepare and stitch the appliqué on to the front rectangle first and then add the backing. There is no batting between the front and back pieces, but some of the appliqué shapes are padded with toy filling.

You should allow 1cm (⅜in) seam allowances throughout on the wallhanging and pockets and 6mm (¼in) seam allowances on the appliqué shapes.

1 Stitching on the borders *From plain fabric:* cut two 65cm (25½in) squares of plain fabric for the front and back. *From patterned fabric:* cut four strips 65 x 6cm (25½ x 2¼in) and four strips 73 x 6cm (28¾ x 2¼in). With right sides together, stitch the shorter strips to the top and bottom edges of the front and back pieces. Press the seams towards the strips. Stitch the long strips to the side edges and press the seams towards the strips.

Preparing the pockets and appliqué

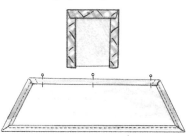

1 Making the house pocket *For the house:* cut a rectangle of fabric 31 x 15.5cm (12¼ x 6¼in). Turn 2cm (¾in) to the wrong side on the long upper edge. Stitch close to the raw edge to hem the pocket. Press a 2cm (¾in) deep pleat 1.5cm (⅝in) in from each short edge. Press under 1cm (⅜in) on the side and lower raw edges, folding the pleats to the wrong side at the lower edge.

2 Adding the door and window *For the door:* cut a rectangle of fabric 10 x 6.5cm (4 x 2½in). *For the window:* cut a rectangle 7 x 6cm (2¾ x 2¼in). Press 6mm (¼in) under on all edges of door and window pieces and pin to the house pocket piece. Slipstitch in place. Using double pink embroidery floss, divide the window into quarters with four straight stitches (see picture on opposite page).

3 Making roof, chimney and smoke Use the traceable pattern to cut a roof from fabric. Press under 1cm (⅜in) on the long and slanted edges and stitch in place. Pin under 1cm (⅜in) on the upper edge. *For the chimney:* cut a 5cm (2in) square of fabric. Press under 6mm (¼in) on three edges of the chimney. Use the traceable pattern to cut out the smoke shape from batting.

4 Making the remaining pockets *For the tractor pocket:* cut a rectangle 14 x 12cm (5½ x 4¾in). *For the hen pocket:* cut a rectangle 26 x 17cm (10¼ x 6¾in). Use the traceable pattern to cut out a basket pocket and a plant pot pocket. Turn under 2cm (¾in) on the upper long edge of the tractor pocket, the upper short edge of the hen pocket and the upper edges of the basket and plant pot pockets. Stitch close to the raw edge. Press under 1cm (⅜in) on the right-hand side and lower edge of the tractor pocket and on all the side and lower edges of the hen, basket and plant pot pockets.

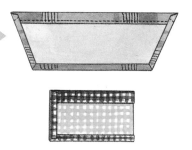

5 Making the tractor cab and sheep patch *For the tractor cab:* cut a rectangle of fabric 18 x 10.5cm (7 x 4¼in). *For the tractor cab window:* cut a rectangle of fabric 7 x 6cm (2¾ x 2¼in). *For the sheep patch:* cut a rectangle of fabric 17 x 14cm (6¾ x 5½in). Press under 6mm (¼in) on all the edges.

6 Making the patterns Cut a 9cm (3½in) diameter circle of paper for the large tractor wheel, a 5.5cm (2⅛in) diameter circle for the small wheel and a 7cm (2¾in) circle for the pig's head. Also cut from paper: two hearts, a tree top, tree trunk, sheep's body, sheep's head, eggs, cat, butterfly, bird, pig's body, pig's muzzle, three tulips and a hen. Pin each paper shape to the wrong side of chosen fabric for that motif. Use the terry cloth for the sheep's body, white fabric for the eggs and pink fabric for the pig's muzzle. Add 6mm (¼in) seam allowances around all shapes and cut out.

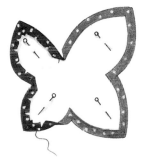

7 Neatening the edges Turn the raw edges of the fabric over the edges of the paper patterns, snipping the curves and inner corners just outside the edges of the paper (leave the short edge of the tree trunk as it will be hidden under the tree top). Cut away the fullness at the corners. Tack in place through the paper. Press the shapes. Carefully remove the tacking and press again. Pull out the paper patterns.

Assembling the hanging

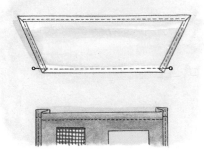

1 Arranging the pieces Refer to the photograph on page 139 to arrange the pieces on the front of the wallhanging. Lap the edge of the roof over the top of the house pocket by 2.5cm (1in). Slip the raw edge of the chimney under the pinned edge of the roof and the raw edge of the trunk under the tree top. Cover the raw edge of the tractor pocket with the cab. Slip the eggs under the top of the basket. Remember to leave space for the basket handle and the tails of the pig and cat. Mark the position of the top of the roof and the hen pocket and basket with pins. Pin all the other pieces in place and pin the hen to the pocket.

3 Stitching the tractor Unpin the right-hand edge of the cab and large wheel and top of the small wheel. Stitch close to the side and lower edges of the pocket. Re-pin the pieces.

▶ *The house in the center of the wallhanging becomes a 'secret' pocket for tiny toys to live in. The roof flap folds down over the opening to hide away treasures.*

2 Stitching the house and roof Stitch close to the side and lower edges of the house pocket. Remove the pins from the roof and open out flat. With the right sides facing, pin the roof to the front, matching the seam allowance to the pin marks. Stitch the roof to the front, catching in the lower edge of the chimney.

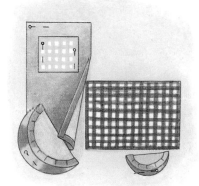

4 Cutting the felt ears and beak Cut two pig's ears from pink felt and a beak for the hen from orange felt. Slip the ears under the pig's head and the beak under the hen's head.

5 Attaching the appliqué pieces Slipstitch the pressed edges of the hearts, tree trunk, sheep patch, eggs, butterfly, bird, tractor cab, tractor window and hen to the background fabric. Stitch the smoke to the top of the chimney with small stitches. Slipstitch the tree top, sheep's body and head, cat, pig's body and head, tractor wheels and tulips, leaving gaps to insert toy filling.

▶ *Polyester toy filling gives the pig a plump, cheeky appeal. The final touch is a fine curly tail made from wool yarn.*

Finishing the design

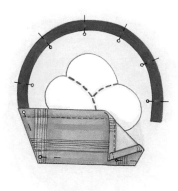

1 Completing the egg basket Using blue embroidery floss, stitch along the broken lines of the eggs with a running stitch. Stretch one edge of the bias binding and arrange in a curve, press to hold the shape. Re-pin the basket in place. Pin the bias binding in a curve as the handle, slipping the ends under the pocket. Slipstitch the handle to the front of the wallhanging. Stitch close to the pressed sides and lower edges of the basket pocket.

2 Stitching the hen pocket Using black embroidery floss, work a French knot for the hen's eye. Using double yellow embroidery floss, work the legs and feet with straight stitches. Re-pin the hen pocket to the front of the wallhanging and stitch close to the pressed sides and lower edges.

3 Padding the shapes Using polyester toy filling, lightly pad shapes through gaps. Slipstitch openings closed.

4 Completing the pig Slipstitch the muzzle to the pig's head. Using double pink embroidery floss, work two straight stitches for each pig's leg. Using black embroidery floss, work French knots for the eyes and nostrils. Thread a large needle with pink wool, knot the end. Bring the thread to the right side at the end of the pig. Arrange the wool in a coil as the tail, catch in place with sewing thread; cut off the excess wool.

5 Completing the sheep and cat Using black embroidery floss, work French knots for the sheep's and cat's eyes and cat's nose. Using double black embroidery floss, work a straight stitch for sheep's legs. Thread a large needle with blue wool and make a tail for the cat in the same way as the pig, arranging the wool in a wavy line.

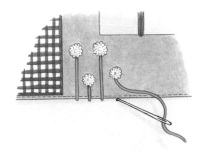

6 Completing fruits, butterfly and flowers Stitch red buttons to tree as fruits. Using double black embroidery floss, work straight stitch for body of butterfly. Arrange four lace flower motifs on basket and house and sew to pockets. Stitch stems of flowers on house with single green floss and tulip stems with double green floss.

Completing the hanging

1 Adding the hanging straps *For the hanging straps:* cut five rectangles of patterned fabric 18 x 10cm (7 x 4in). Fold lengthways in half with right sides facing. Stitch the long edges. Turn right side out and press. Fold the straps in half, matching the raw edges. Tack two straps to the top of the front wallhanging 1cm (³⁄₈in) inside the outer edges. Space the remaining straps evenly along the top edge and tack in place.

2 Finishing the wallhanging With right sides facing, stitch the front and back pieces of the wallhanging together, leaving a 30cm (12in) gap on the lower edge. Snip the seam allowances across the corners, turn right side out and slipstitch the opening closed. Saw the broomstick to 78cm (31in) and paint it red. Leave to dry then slip the broomstick through the straps. Cut two flowers from orange felt and two centers from pink felt. Glue the centers to the flowers. Glue the flowers to the ends of the broomstick.

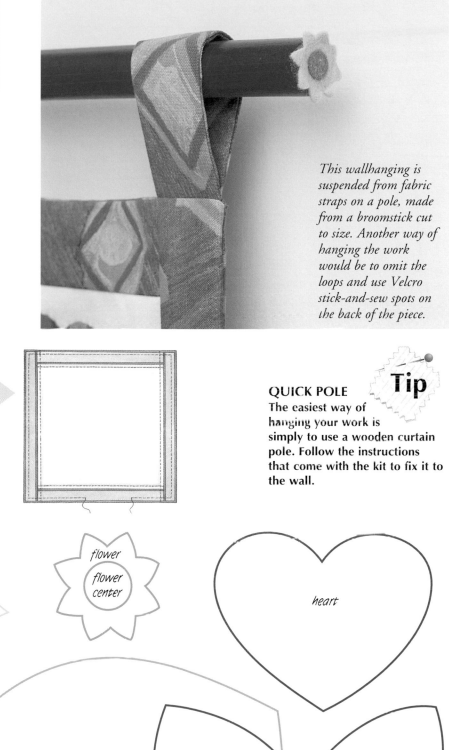

This wallhanging is suspended from fabric straps on a pole, made from a broomstick cut to size. Another way of hanging the work would be to omit the loops and use Velcro stick-and-sew spots on the back of the piece.

QUICK POLE **Tip**
The easiest way of hanging your work is simply to use a wooden curtain pole. Follow the instructions that come with the kit to fix it to the wall.

Traceable patterns

flower

flower center

heart

bird

cat

butterfly

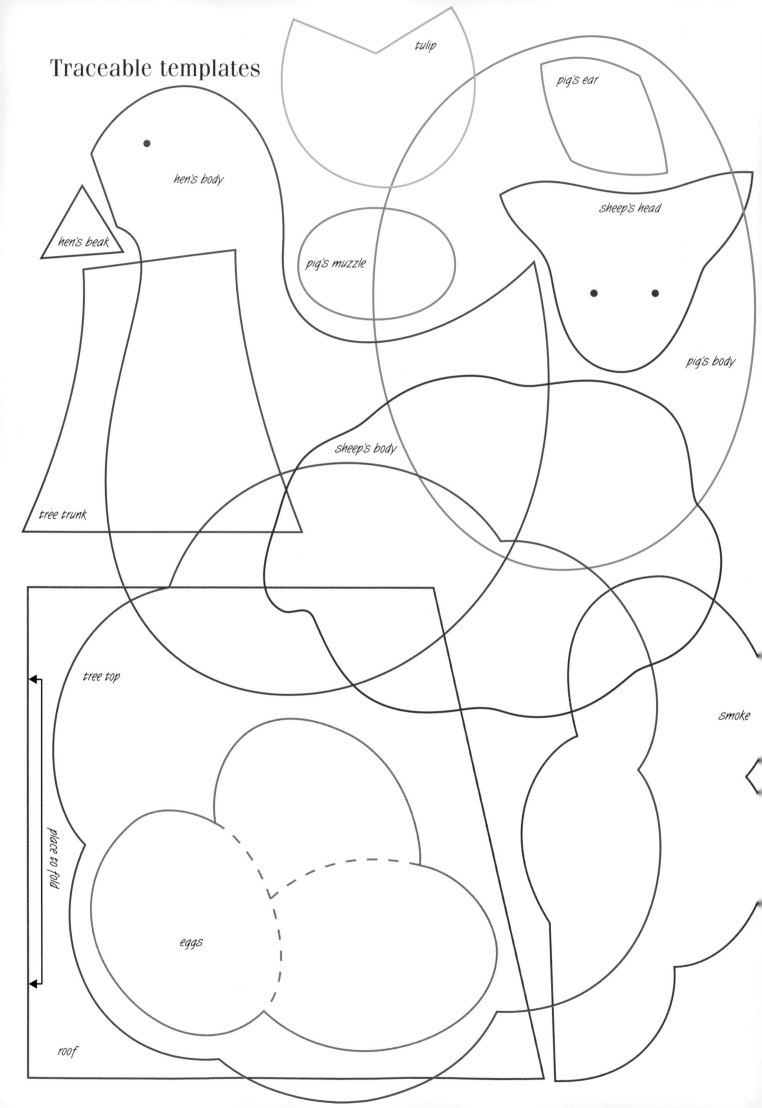

Traceable templates

tulip

pig's ear

hen's body

sheep's head

hen's beak

pig's muzzle

pig's body

sheep's body

tree trunk

smoke

tree top

place to fold

eggs

roof

Patchwork crib quilt

*By machine stitching squares of coordinating
fabrics together you can make an original patchwork crib quilt
to celebrate a new baby's arrival.*

Machine stitching squares of fabric together is the simplest way to create attractive and original patchwork patterns. When designing patchwork, it is important to choose fabrics which go well together. A mixture of patterned and plain, floral and geometric prints is often used. For a clear design, do not be tempted to use too many different patterns in one piece of patchwork. To make each of the quilts shown here, you need only four different color-coordinated fabrics, one of which is plain.

For a crib quilt, it is essential that all the fabrics and the batting are washable. You should also check that all the fabrics are pre-shrunk.

Choose fabrics which go well in the baby's room. You can incorporate the

▲ *Clowns cartwheeling over a colorful patchwork crib quilt bring all the fun of the circus leaping into the nursery.*

curtain fabric into the patchwork design, or use one of your chosen prints for other items in the room – a lampshade, a cushion cover or a laundry bag, for example.

Cutting the patches

The finished size of the quilt (including border) is 80.5 x 103.5cm (31½ x 40½in) to fit a standard crib, while the stitched size of each patch is 11.5cm (4½in) square.

It is important to cut the patches accurately with the same seam allowance, so that when you stitch them together the seamlines all meet and match. To get any bold motifs in the center of the patch, use a template as a cutting guide.

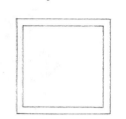

1 Drawing up the patch template On a sheet of tracing paper, draw an accurate 13.5cm (5¼in) square. Draw another line 1cm (⅜in) inside the first square to mark the stitching line and finished size of the patch.

2 Cutting out motifs from fabric A Making sure that the motif falls in the center of the patch, pin the template in position on the fabric and cut around it, always making sure that the edges of the template are parallel to the straight grain of the fabric. Repeat to cut a total of 17 picture patches.

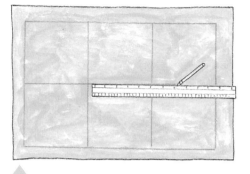

3 Cutting patches B, C and D Mark 13.5cm (5¼in) squares accurately on the wrong side of the three remaining fabrics with the water-soluble pen. Cut six patches from each, including the border fabric.

You will need

- ◆ 75cm (30in) fabric with the main motif (A)
- ◆ 2m (2¼yd) fabric (B) 122cm (48in) wide, for patches, borders and back of quilt
- ◆ 30cm (⅓yd) each of other two fabrics (C and D) for patches
- ◆ 110cm (1⅔yd) of 90cm (36in) wide 100g (4oz) washable polyester batting
- ◆ Tracing paper and pencil
- ◆ Water-soluble pen
- ◆ Ruler
- ◆ Matching sewing thread
- ◆ Needle and dressmaking pins

Stitching the patchwork

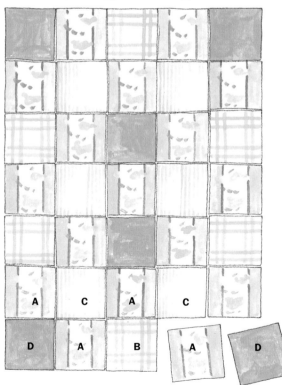

1 Arranging the pieces Following the diagram above, lay the patches out on a table with five squares across and seven squares down, placing them so that the same fabric does not join up horizontally or vertically.

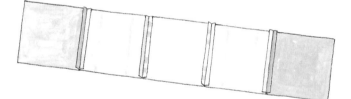

2 Joining the patches into strips With right sides together, pin and stitch the patches in the correct order in strips of five, taking 1cm (⅜in) seam allowances. Trim the seam allowances to 6mm (¼in) and press the seams open.

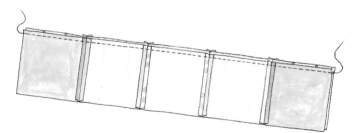

3 Stitching the strips together Stitch the patch strips together, making sure that they are in the right order. Trim seam allowances and press seams open.

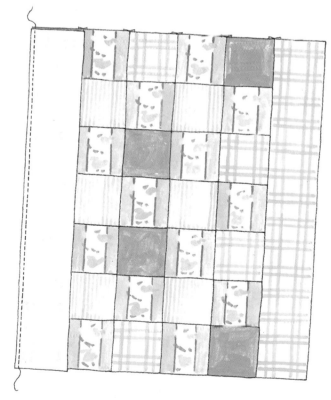

▲ *The duck patches look cute interspersed among the coordinating plain, striped and checked fabrics. For ease, select fabrics like these from a coordinating range.*

4 Attaching the long borders Measure the longest side of the patchwork, and cut two strips of fabric **B** the same length and 13.5cm (5¼in) wide. Pin and machine in place. Trim seam allowances and press seams open.

5 Attaching the short borders Measure the shorter sides, including the borders, and cut two strips of **B** this length and 13.5cm (5¼in) wide. Pin and machine in place. Trim seam allowances and press seams open.

Making up the quilt

1 Cutting out the backing and batting Measure the finished piece of patchwork, including the borders, and cut the backing fabric (**B**) to the same size. Cut a piece of batting to the same size as well.

25cm (10in)

2 Joining the layers together Place the patchwork and backing fabric right sides together. Lay the batting on top and pin through all layers. Tack, then machine together with a 1cm (³⁄₈in) seam allowance all around, leaving a 25cm (10in) gap in the stitching along the bottom edge.

◀ *When it is not being used as bedding, a teddy bear crib quilt makes a cheerful wallhanging for a baby's room.*

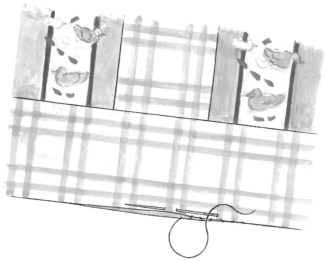

3 Stitching the opening Turn the quilt right sides out through the opening. Slipstitch the opening to join the two folded edges together invisibly. Press with a cool iron.

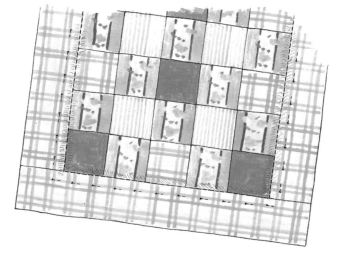

4 Quilting the cover Pin through all layers along the edge of the central patchwork panel. Machine stitch along the seamline to give the border a quilted effect.

Kids' dice seats

*Toddler-sized cubes filled with polystyrene bead
filling make useful impromptu seating for a playroom and, with
their appliquéd dice markings, double as fun toys.*

These cheery looking dice with their bright colors and dots make great toys for small children, encouraging their counting skills and color recognition. They also make a fun accessory for board games – a small child can easily toss the dice, because they are filled with lightweight polystyrene beads, and they make a handy little perch for a toddler too.

Make one to fit in a corner, or two or three to pile up mixing up a bright selection of colors. For an alternative look, make the dice in black and add brightly colored spots, or leave out the spots altogether and use up scraps of

▲ *Small children will love these colorful soft cube seats which they can also use as building blocks or bean bags to sit on or throw around.*

furnishing fabric to make coordinating seating that tones with the color scheme of the room.

Making a dice seat

Choose a strong furnishing fabric for the cover of the dice seat. The covers are zipped around two sides to give easy access to the inner calico lining. For the fabric circles, a wine glass or mug base makes a good template.

You will need

- ◆ **0.7m (³/₄yd) furnishing fabric**
- ◆ **Contrast fabric for dots**
- ◆ **0.7m (³/₄yd) calico**
- ◆ **Bonding fabric such as WonderUnder**
- ◆ **55cm (21¹/₂in) zipper**
- ◆ **Matching thread**
- ◆ **Polystyrene bead filling**
- ◆ **Zipper foot**
- ◆ **Wine glass or small mug**

1 Cutting out *For each cube:* cut six squares 33cm (13in) square.

2 Adding the dots Apply the bonding fabric to the back of the contrast fabric (see page 74), then cut 21 circles 2-2.5cm (³/₄-1in) in diameter. Position the dots on each square as on a dice, iron on and stitch in place, using an open zigzag stitch.

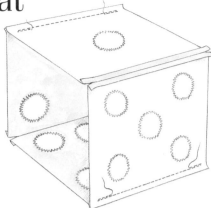

3 Joining the sides Right sides together, join four squares to make a loop of fabric for the sides, like a dice, leaving 1.5cm (⁵/₈in) open at each end of the seams. Press seams open.

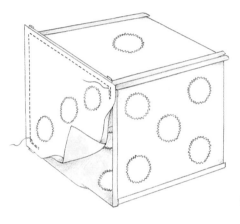

4 Fitting the base Right sides together, pin the base square to the lower edges of two adjoining sides. Continue pinning 2.5cm (1in) into the other two squares, but leave the rest open. Stitch, backstitching at each end for strength. Press under seam allowances on the open section.

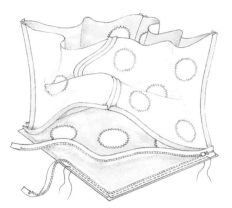

5 Starting the zipper Open the zipper. Center one side face down on the opened seam allowance, with the teeth on the pressed seamline. At the corner, snip into tape so that it lies flat. Pin and stitch close to the pressed seamline, using a zipper foot. Turn the allowance under.

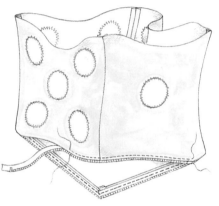

6 Completing the zipper Lap the other pressed seam allowance over the free side of the zipper, with the fold on the teeth. Pin, and stitch 6mm (¹/₄in) from the fold.

7 Adding the top square Right sides together, pin and stitch top square to the top edges of the side squares.

8 Making the lining *From the calico:* cut out six 34cm (13¹/₂in) squares. Stitch together as for the main cover, omitting the zipper and leaving a 7.5cm (3in) gap in one seam.

9 Filling the lining Make a funnel from a rolled-up newspaper or piece of card and then, using a ladle, fill the cube with bead filling. Slipstitch closed and insert the lining into the cover.

◀ *Applying a long zipper right along two sides of the cube means that the covers can easily be removed for cleaning.*

Chairs for children

A bright and colorful, covered foam chair, that can
be turned into a spare bed at a moment's notice, is a fun way
of providing versatile furniture for a child's room.

Furnishing a growing child's room can be a costly business, especially when you want to provide for lots of different activities besides sleeping. Most children like to have a chair which is just for them – to curl up in with a book, watch television or just daydream. This cosy chair, however, also provides for the inevitable friend staying over – it can be unfolded to make two separate floor cushions, or a comfortable mattress long enough for a child up to 10 years old. The separate roly-poly bolster makes a fun addition to the play area.

All the pieces are held together with sturdy Velcro-backed tabs, so you can put them together to create different combinations – stack three cushions instead of two, for example, for a higher chair. The cushions are cut from foam, so they are light enough for a child to move easily, and zippers ensure that the covers can be removed quickly and easily for washing. The bolster is simply a long roll of batting, covered with a cylinder of fabric and gathered in with elastic through casings at each end.

▼ *This stack-it-yourself chair is fun for children, as well as being practical as a spare bed for when young friends come to stay. Velcro tabs, which can be pulled apart easily, hold the cushions together.*

Making the gusset cushions

Choose a robust, washable fabric, such as canvas or calico, at least 125cm (49½in) wide. Mix and match plains or patterns to suit your color scheme. The covers are cut slightly smaller than the foam for a snug fit, and the zippers in the gussets wrap around each side by 7.5cm (3in) to make the covers easier to remove for cleaning. Some fabric stores sell zippers by the meter (yard) – ask for it to be cut to the length required, then stitch across the teeth at the base to form a bottom stop. Alternatively, you can buy two zippers to make up the required length, and insert them to meet in the middle.

Ask a foam supplier to cut the seat slabs for you in a medium density foam. The rolled batting for the bolster is calculated on a standard width of 96cm (37¾in). If you use a narrower batting, you will have to work out how much extra you need to buy.

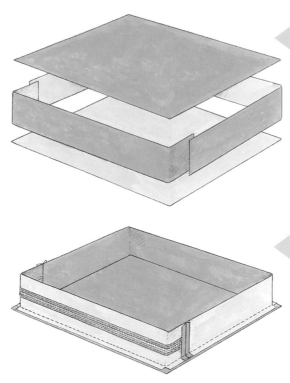

You will need

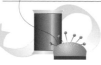

For two cushions:

◆ **3m (3¹/₃yd) of 125cm (49½in) wide furnishing fabric for two gusset cushions (or 2m [2¹/₄yd] for a single cushion)**

◆ **2m (2¹/₄yd) of 125cm (49½in) wide furnishing fabric for the bolster**

◆ **3.6m (3yd) of heavyweight batting**

◆ **25cm (¹/₃yd) of contrast fabric for the tabs**

◆ **3.2m (3⁵/₈yd) of 2.5cm (1in) wide Velcro**

◆ **Two zippers, 100cm (39in) long**

◆ **1m (1¹/₈yd) of 6mm (¹/₄in) wide elastic**

◆ **Matching thread**

◆ **Two foam slabs, 15cm (6in) thick by 84cm (33in) long by 62cm (24½in) wide**

3 Cutting the Velcro Cut the hard and soft sides of the Velcro into sixteen equal pieces, each 20cm (8in) long. Then separate the strips, putting the hard Velcro aside for the tabs.

▼ *Laid end-to-end, the cushions make a bed for a friend to stay overnight; turn it into a sofa bed with the bolster against the wall for a comfortable back rest.*

1 Cutting the base covers Cut out the following pieces for each gusset cushion: *for the top and bottom,* cut two rectangles 86 x 64cm (33 x 24¾in); *for the main gusset panel,* cut one strip 195 x 17cm (76¼ x 6¾in); *for the zipper gusset panel,* cut one strip 101 x 20cm (39¾ x 8in).

2 Starting the cushions Cut the zipper panel in half lengthways and tack together again with right sides facing, taking a 1.5cm (⁵/₈in) seam allowance. Press the seam open and center it over the right side of the zipper. Pin and stitch down each side, using a zipper foot 6mm (¼in) from the center seam. Unpick the tacking stitches. Right sides together, pin and stitch the short ends of the main gusset piece to short ends of zipper panel taking 1.5cm (⁵/₈in) seams. This makes a continuous piece. Press seams open. Tack gusset at corner positions. With right sides together, center zipper section of the gusset on back edge of bottom piece. Continue pinning all around, clipping gusset seam allowance at the corners. Stitch. Repeat to start the second cushion.

4 Attaching soft side of Velcro On the top cushion, center wrong side of a soft Velcro strip to the right side of the back (zipper panel) edge and each side of the gusset, 1.5cm (⅝in) below the top seamline. Pin in place. On top piece of the cushion, center one piece of Velcro 20cm (8in) in from the stitching line at each side edge, and another 15cm (6in) in from the back edge. Also on the top cushion, center two more pieces 1.5cm (⅝in) above lower seamline at the back and the front of the gusset.

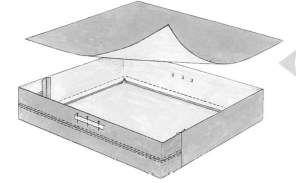

5 Positioning the lower Velcro On the bottom cushion, center the wrong side of a soft Velcro strip on to the right side of the cushion at the front and back, 1.5cm (⅝in) down from the top seamline.

6 Stitching the Velcro Machine stitch round all four sides of each Velcro strip.

7 Completing the covers Attach the top section of the cushion in the same way as the bottom (see step **2**), lining up the top and bottom pieces carefully. Neaten the raw edges with zigzag stitch. Turn to the right side. Roll up the foam slab and insert carefully through the zipper. Smooth out.

8 Making the tabs From contrast fabric, cut eight rectangles 24 x 18cm (8½ x 7in). Right sides together and taking a 1cm (⅜in) seam allowance, stitch long edges of each piece together, leaving a 5cm (2in) opening in the middle. Center seam along strip and press open. Stitch across the short ends, then turn to the right side and press.

9 Adding hard side of Velcro On each tab, center one strip of the hard Velcro each side of the center seam; stitch round all four sides to secure.

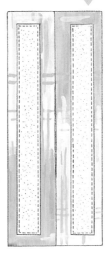

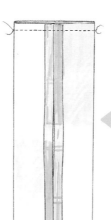

Making the bolster

The bolster forms the back and 'arms' of the chair, and is held in place by Velcro tabs. The bolster is very easy to make: the batting is rolled up to form a sausage and the ends of the fabric cover are secured with an elastic casing.

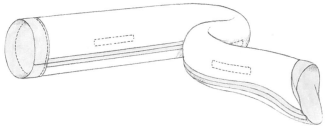

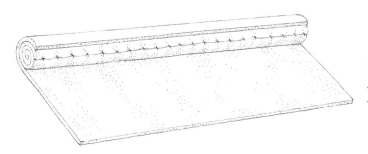

1 Making the pad Cut two lengths of batting 180cm (71in) long. Starting from one long edge, roll up one length to make a sausage, oversewing the edge with large stitches to secure. Roll this up in the next length, rolling firmly but not too tightly. Continue until the roll is 20cm (8in) in diameter, oversewing the edge to finish.

3 Stitching the bolster cover Pin fabric round bolster and place on top cushion to check Velcro positions. Alter position of Velcro if necessary, then stitch as in step **6** on page 153. Fold cover in half, right sides and long edges together. Stitch long edges; press seam open. At each end, turn under 1.5cm (⅝in) then 2.5cm (1in); stitch close to fold.

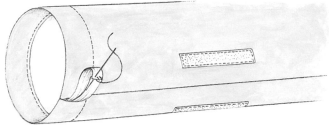

2 Cutting the bolster cover From the bolster fabric, cut a rectangle 208 x 68cm (80⅝ x 26¾in). On the right side, and starting 34cm (13⅜in) from one end, pin two strips of soft Velcro parallel, 11.5cm (4½in) in from the long sides. Repeat at the other end. Pin the remaining two pieces centrally in line with the other pairs.

4 Inserting the elastic On the right side, at each end of the cover, open the seam slightly where it crosses the casing; neaten the ends. Cut the elastic in half and thread it through the casing at each end, securing the loose end of elastic with a safety pin. Stitch ends together securely.

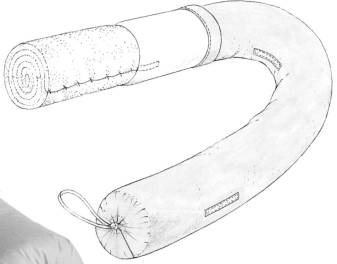

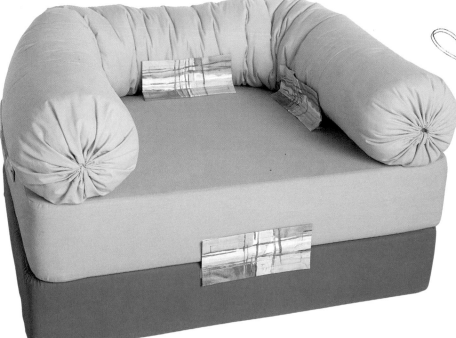

5 Inserting the pad Turn the cover inside out, turning in one end a short way. Push the pad in this end, then roll the rest of the cover over the pad. Pull the elastic tight at each end of the bolster and knot to secure; tuck the remaining loop out of sight inside the casing.

◄ *Choose washable, sturdy cottons in contrasting plain colors for the cushion and bolster covers, and splashy prints for the Velcro tabs.*

Bean bags

*A squashy, inviting bean bag makes ideal casual seating
anywhere in the home; perfect for children of all ages to snuggle
into, it makes an equally suitable bed for a pet.*

Filled with a polybead filling, this generously proportioned bean bag has a novelty appeal for most youngsters who enjoy the way the beads mold around their shape. It makes a portable, flexible place to relax and, with its built-in handle, even a small child can drag this colorful and light-weight bag around .

Polybeads are made of polystyrene, which is a non-allergenic material, and the outer cover has a zipper so it is easy to remove the filling when the bag needs washing. These two aspects make the bean bag a healthy alternative to conventional seating for children with allergy problems. Make one to pamper your pet and it will help preserve your sofa and chairs, as well as confine the animal hairs to one easily cleaned item.

Choose a tough, washable fabric for the cover, with a cheerful cartoon print for small children. Bright stripes and checks coordinate well in an otherwise plain room and will also be popular with older children. For a novel effect, make one up in a glamorous fake fur zebra or leopard print to grace your sitting room.

▼ *With its soft and welcoming look, this bean bag offers a comfortable, relaxing alternative to a chair or bed. Put one in the corner of a child's room, to make a cosy, peaceful spot for reading quietly or playing with a favorite cuddly toy.*

Making a bean bag

This bean bag has a washable cover, double stitched for strength, and a calico inner lining for the polybead filling. You can buy bags of polybead filling from craft stores. Two to three bags of two cubic feet should be enough to fill the bean bag; save any left over to top up the bag when the beads become flattened through prolonged use.

You will need

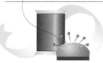

- ◆ **3.5m (3⁷/₈yd) of furnishing fabric**
- ◆ **3.5m (3⁷/₈yd) of calico**
- ◆ **Scrap of mediumweight fusible interfacing**
- ◆ **Matching thread**
- ◆ **40cm (16in) zipper**
- ◆ **Polybead filling**
- ◆ **Large sheets of paper**
- ◆ **Ruler and pencil**

▼ *Complete with its own handle, the bean bag can be moved around easily, or even stored on a hook to leave the floor clear for playing.*

1 Making the side pattern Cut a piece of paper 95 x 50cm (37½ x 19¾in); fold in half lengthways. At the bottom edge, mark 14cm (5½in) from the fold (**A**), then mark the top edge 6cm (2¼in) from the fold (**B**). Mark the outer edge 33cm (13in) from the bottom (**C**). Join **A** and **B** to **C**. Trim away the surplus paper.

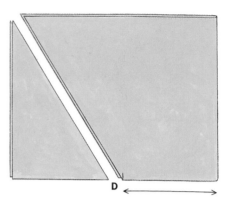

2 Making the base pattern Cut a piece of paper 56 x 24cm (22 x 9½in); fold it in half widthways. On the bottom edge, measure and mark 14cm (5½in) from the fold (**D**). Draw a line from this point to the top outer corner. Trim away surplus.

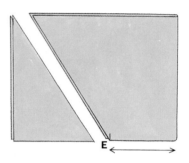

3 Making the top pattern Cut a piece of paper 24 x 10.5cm (9½ x 4⅛in); fold it in half widthways. Measure and mark the bottom edge 6cm (2¼in) in from the fold (**E**). Draw a line from this point to the top outer corner. Trim away the surplus paper.

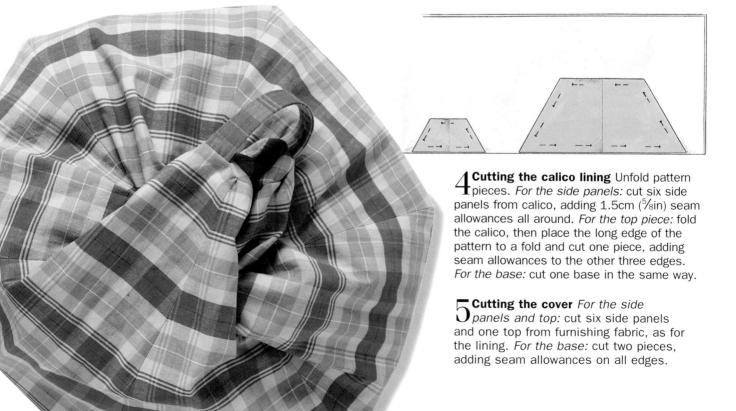

4 Cutting the calico lining Unfold pattern pieces. *For the side panels:* cut six side panels from calico, adding 1.5cm (⅝in) seam allowances all around. *For the top piece:* fold the calico, then place the long edge of the pattern to a fold and cut one piece, adding seam allowances to the other three edges. *For the base:* cut one base in the same way.

5 Cutting the cover *For the side panels and top:* cut six side panels and one top from furnishing fabric, as for the lining. *For the base:* cut two pieces, adding seam allowances on all edges.

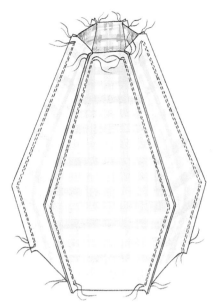

6 Stitching the cover sides With right sides together, pin and stitch the long edges of all the side panels to form a tube shape, beginning and ending each seam 1.5cm (⅝in) in from the ends. Stitch again for strength, then neaten and press the seams open.

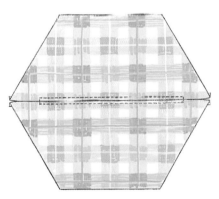

7 Inserting the zipper Pin long edges of base pieces right sides together, then stitch 9cm (3½in) in from each side edge, leaving an opening in the center. Press the seam open, then insert the zipper.

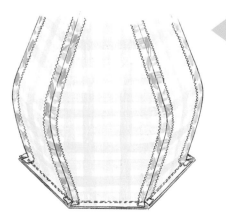

The hexagonal construction of the bean bag creates interesting patterns with checks or stripes – for the best effect, match the pattern at the seams.

8 Attaching the base With right sides and raw edges together, pin the base to bottom edge of the tube shape, matching the seams to the points of the base. The unstitched ends of the seams will splay out to ease the fit. Stitch twice to reinforce seam; neaten seam.

9 Making the handle *From both furnishing fabric and interfacing:* cut a rectangle 30 x 14cm (12 x 5½in). Fuse the interfacing to the wrong side of the fabric. Fold the fabric in half lengthways, with right sides together; stitch 1cm (⅜in) from the long edges. Turn the handle to the right side, center the seam, then stitch close to the folds on each side.

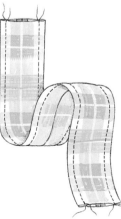

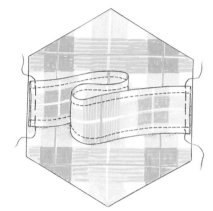

12 Making the lining Pin and stitch the lining side panels together as for the main cover, leaving a 20cm (8in) gap in one seam for filling the bean bag. Pin and stitch the base and top sections in place as before, omitting the zipper and the handle. Turn the lining through to the right side.

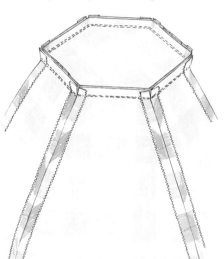

10 Attaching the handle Right side up, center the handle across the top piece, matching the raw edges. Tack the ends in place at the sides.

11 Adding the top piece Open zipper. With right sides together, pin edges of the top piece to top edges of side panels as for base, sandwiching handle edges between. Stitch seam twice to reinforce seam; neaten seam. Turn cover to right side.

13 Adding the filling Use a ladle or scoop and a paper funnel to pour the beads into the lining. Fill the shape to about two-thirds of its total height; slipstitch the opening closed. Insert the filled lining into the cover and shake it into place.

▼ *Coordinate your bean bag with other soft furnishings – here a fun animal print looks bright and fresh.*

INDEX

PICTURE ACKNOWLEDGMENTS

Photographs: Laura Ashley 8(tl), 14(tl); Biggie Best 23(tr); Jane Churchill 12(bl), 46(b); CPi 92, 93(t,b), 94(tr,b), 95(b), 96, 98(tbl); Crowson Fabrics 112(t); The Dormy House 112(c); Eaglemoss Publications (Paul Bricknell) 13(bl), 14(b), 18, 53(c), (Martin Chaffer) 103(l), (Jez Hawley) 55(t), (Lizzie Orme) 58, 59(b), 99(b), 100(b), 102(b), 119, 123, 131(b,c), 133(b), 134(t), (Graham Rae) 33(c), 50(bl), 68(br), 90, 117(c), 128(bl), 156(bl), 157(t), (Gareth Sambidge) 89(c), (George Talyor) 26(t), (Steve Tanner) 31(br), 32(tr), 62(tr,b), 91(b), 103(r), 104(t), 145(c), 147(t), 148(tl), (Adrian Taylor) 137(br), 151, (George Taylor) 20(t), 25(c), 28(t), 34(t), 36(t), 63(c), 64(c,bl,bc,br), 65(tl,tr,b), 69(c), 71(tr), 77, 80, 81(b), 82(bl), 113(c), 114(tr), 116(tr), 139(l), 141(b), 142(t), 143(tr), 149(c), 150(bl); Anna French 137(bl); Hamerville Magazines Ltd 91(r), 111(br); Robert Harding Syndication

(Sian Irvine/Inspirations) 8(bl), (Steven Pam/Inspirations) 22(bl); IPC Syndication (Country Homes & Interiors) 11(c), 12(tr), 14(tr), 29(c), (Homes & Gardens) 7(c), 9(t,b), 10(tr), 13(br), 16(l), 56(b), 84(br), 108(c), 109(c), (Homes & Ideas) 83(l,r), 111(t), (Ideal Home) 10(br), 15(c), 110(bl), (Woman & Home) 13(tr), 61(c), (Jan Baldwin/Country Homes & Interiors) 51(c), 52(tr), (Jan Baldwin/Homes & Gardens) 37(l), 107(b), (Jan Baldwin/Ideal Home) 127(l), (Jan Baldwin/Options) 106(b), (David Barrett/Homes & Gardens) 130(tr), (Bill Batten/Country Homes & Interiors) 110(b), (Dominic Blackmore/Homes & Ideas) 130(b), 136(tr,bl), 137(t), 138(bl,br), 158(b), (Dominic Blackmore/Ideal Home) 108(t), (Simon Brown/Ideal Home) 47(b), (Harry Cory-Wright/Homes & Gardens) 49(t), (Country Homes & Interiors/Polly Wreford) 138(tr), (Chris Drake/Country

Homes & Interiors) 107(t), (Chris Drake/Homes & Gardens) 67(l), 68(l), (Richard Foster/Homes & Gardens) 98(br), (Tom Leighton/Homes & Gardens) 105(c), (James Merrell/Homes & Gardens) 106(br), Osborne & Little 135(c); Romo Ltd 17(c); VNU Syndication 19(l), 39(t), 41(t), 59(t), 68(tr), 73(c), 75(cr), 76(tr), 110(tl), 155(b), (Ariadne Holland) 16(r), 108(b), (Doe Het Zelf) 94(tl), (Margriet) 106(t); Elizabeth Whiting & Associates (Michael Dunne) 8(br), 24(bl), (Gary Chowanetz) 85(c), (Rodney Hyett) 87(tr), (Di Lewis) 21(c), 43(c), 57(c), 60(bl), (Andreas von Einsiedel) 10(bl), 45(t).

Illustrations: John Hutchinson 22, 26, 30, 34, 38, 44, 48, 54, 60(tr), 86, 104, 112(b), 114, 118, 120, 128, 132, 145, 150, 152, 156; Coral Mula 20(b), 52(b), 58(t), 59(bl), 70, 74, 78, 82, 84, 100, 124, 140; Patrick Mulrey 144.